THE CHINESE MENU COOKBOOK

including an introductory course in Chinese cooking

JOANNE HUSH
and PETER WONG

An Owl Book

HOLT, RINEHART and WINSTON
New York

Published by Holt, Rinehart and Winston,
383 Madison Avenue, New York, New York 10017.

Published simultaneously in Canada by Holt, Rinehart and Winston
of Canada, Limited.

Library of Congress Cataloging in Publication Data

Hush, Joanne.
The Chinese menu cookbook.

Includes index.
1.   Cookery, Chinese.   I.   Wong, Peter, joint author.
II.   Title.
TX724.5.C5H87   1976   641.5′951   75-21469

ISBN Hardbound: 0 – 03 – 014931 – 2
ISBN Paperback: 0 – 03 – 044776 – 3

First Holt Paperback Edition – 1978

Drawings by Valerie Mason
Designer: The Etheredges
Printed in the United States of America
10 9 8 7 6 5

ISBN 0-03-014931-2 HARDBOUND
ISBN 0-03-044776-3 PAPERBACK

THE
CHINESE
MENU
COOKBOOK

To my husband Paul, who had the idea for this book and helped me with it, and our children—Jamie, the best fourteen-year-old chef anywhere, and Jeffrey, Mike, and Katie, who are most enthusiastic recipe tasters.

J.H.

To my wife and family, to my friend, Ken Martin, who helped greatly with the recipes, and to chef Alex Wong and the staffs at the Mandarin Inn restaurants.

P.W.

CONTENTS

MORE MENUS
Additional Balanced Menus for All Tastes and Occasions

MORE RECIPES

Recipes You Can Substitute in Our Suggested Menus and
from Which You Can Make Up Your Own Menus

THE
CHINESE
MENU
COOKBOOK

ABOUT
CHINESE COOKING
AND THIS BOOK

The first thing to know about Chinese cooking is that you really *can* learn to do it well on your own. With no more than this book to start and a reasonable amount of diligence, you will be cooking great Chinese meals in a remarkably short time.

In fact, Chinese cooking is less complicated than the two other great national cuisines, French and Italian. There are some basic new techniques to learn—in both preparation and cooking —but you will learn these quickly. There are some new ingredients to get used to—fewer, though, than you might think; vegetables and condiments primarily—and some will take just a little effort to find. There is some new equipment you will want, but not much—a wok, a cleaver, possibly a steamer—and even these are not absolutely essential. Chinese cooking does take more preparation time (but less cooking time) than you generally will have been used to. There are things that will be new, but there is absolutely nothing about any of it that need intimidate you.

If your main exposure to Chinese food has been with takeout egg rolls or frozen supermarket "chow mein," we can promise you that the meals you will soon be preparing will be a revelation to you. Or, if you think the only good Chinese food is at your favorite Chinese restaurant, you will soon discover a new favorite spot—your own kitchen. You have nothing less than a great food experience ahead of you.

As if that weren't enough, you will find that Chinese cooking has the additional virtues of being especially nutritious, economical, and creative. Nutritious because it uses many vegetables, is low in carbohydrates, and specializes in fast cooking which helps to retain vitamins and nutrients. Economical because Chinese recipes do not generally require expensive cuts of meat and the individual dishes use smaller portions of meat than do American recipes. Creative because you have an almost unlimited variety in the dishes you can combine in one meal, including recipe versions you can improvise yourself.

Many of the recipes in this book are specialties of the popular Mandarin Inn restaurants in New York's Chinatown, owned by coauthor Peter Wong. Born in mainland China, Peter went with his family to Hong Kong before coming to the United States in 1960. He opened his first restaurant at 14 Mott Street in New York in 1970, specializing in Peking and Szechuan cooking. A feature of the restaurant has been Peter's Sunday afternoon cooking demonstrations. The success of the first Mandarin Inn led in 1974 to the opening of the second, located almost around the corner on Pell Street.

Other recipes in the book are used by coauthor Joanne Hush in the Chinese cooking courses she teaches in Fairfield County, Connecticut. The menu planning, the lesson program, and the special organization of recipes followed in this book are based on these courses. Joanne studied Chinese cooking at the China Institute in New York and with other teachers in the city.

Joanne and Peter met several years ago as a result of a number of superb dinners at the Mandarin Inn and because of their mutual interests in good Chinese cooking and in teaching.

Joanne began to bring her cooking classes there for a special banquet at the end of each course.

During this time Peter and Joanne became friends, and out of their friendship came the plan for collaborating on a book that would bring together his extensive cooking experience and great recipes, and her menu-oriented teaching approach to encourage even the most timid cook to try home-cooked Chinese meals.

Menu planning is more intricate and probably more important in Chinese meals than in any other kind of cooking.

In Western cooking a dinner is generally built around a single main dish supplemented by vegetables, a salad, possibly a preliminary course, and often ending with dessert. The *quantity* of a dish varies with the number of people to be served, but the *number* of different dishes doesn't change appreciably.

In Chinese cooking it is quite different. The amount made of a given dish (particularly most stir-fried dishes) does not change substantially, no matter how many people are to be served. Instead, the number of dishes is increased as the number of people increases. A general rule of thumb would be to have one dish on the menu for each person at the meal (not including rice)—thus, two dishes (plus rice) for two persons, six dishes for six persons.

One major reason the Chinese increase the number of dishes in proportion to the number of people instead of increasing the quantity of each dish is the very nature of stir-fry cooking in a wok. You just can't double or triple a stir-fry recipe and get the same results. If there is too much food in a wok it won't cook quickly; the vegetables won't stay crisp, and the meat will become soggy and overdone. From this practical limitation and long centuries of evolving tradition, the Chinese have come to favor the great diversity in the planning of their special meals that makes their cuisine so unique.

This diversity, however, raises a very practical problem for the beginner in Chinese cooking. How can she (or he) plan a meal that is not only good on the table, but manageable in the kitchen and made with ingredients that can be found without unreasonable effort?

This book is specifically designed to answer this need. We have given particular attention to planning menus for balance. Balance not only in the sense that the foods go well together and look well together—a pleasing variety of color and texture and taste—but also, very importantly, balanced in the demands the meal makes on the cook, so that not too many dishes in any meal require last-minute stir-frying or excessive advance preparation. It is as important for you to enjoy the cooking of a Chinese meal as it is for your family and guests to enjoy the eating of it.

We also have tried to structure the recipes in this book in ways that should make their preparation easier for you. When certain ingredients in a recipe are to be combined prior to the final cooking—a sauce, a vegetable mixture, a special marinade— these ingredients are grouped and separately identified in the recipe, and then placed in individual bowls on a tray ready for cooking.

In all the recipes in this book we indicate approximately how much preparation and cooking time is required, and if it can be prepared in advance and be refrigerated or frozen. We also give the regional derivation of major dishes so that you will learn the distinguishing differences among the cuisines of China.

Finally, and importantly, we have made a special effort to select recipes whose ingredients can be easily found in most communities. In a separate section on ingredients we discuss where each basic Chinese ingredient can be found, what to look for when buying it, and how to store it. We also list possible substitutions for some relatively harder-to-find items.

In the following pages we will discuss first the equipment, ingredients, and techniques you will need to know about. Then our series of six menu lessons will take you step by step through an introductory course in Chinese cooking. New techniques are introduced as the lessons progress, and a variety of ingredients are included so that you will quickly become familiar with the basic Chinese cooking methods and foods. We will begin with a very simple dinner for two and build your skills until you can tackle, with confidence, a multidish "banquet" for eight.

Later in the book we include a further series of balanced menus that you will be ready for when you have completed the first menus. Following that there are a number of other recipes from which you can create your own menus or substitute dishes for those we have included in our menu section.

To help the beginner we have given full and detailed instructions on the preparation and cooking and serving techniques used by the Chinese cook. But this book is not for the novice alone. If you have already mastered the basic techniques, you can scan these instructions and use the book for its other primary purpose —to offer you a varied selection of our favorite recipes brought together in balanced menus that we believe will help you better to organize, and even better to enjoy, your own Chinese cooking.

GETTING READY

EQUIPMENT

It is fully possible for you to prepare Chinese meals with the cooking utensils you now have in your kitchen. You can use a regular skillet for stir-fry dishes, an electric frying pan for deep-fat frying, and a simple device for steaming that we will describe on page 14. You can use a standard kitchen spoon and spatula for stirring, and your heaviest kitchen knife for slicing and chopping. So you don't have to buy any new equipment, and you may, indeed, want to start out without doing so.

However, it is better if you can soon acquire a wok and the special Chinese cleaver. These implements will make Chinese cooking easier for you and we do recommend that you have them. Not only are the wok and cleaver uniquely suited to the techniques of Chinese cooking, but you simply will feel more like a Chinese cook and, thus, operate with more confidence if you use them.

In due course you may want to acquire a bamboo steamer and some specially designed stirring implements, but these are not essential at the beginning. In any case, as you will see, none of these things are particularly expensive.

Here are the standard Chinese cooking implements:

WOK

The wok is a round-bottomed pan used primarily for stir-fry cooking, the most important of Chinese cooking methods. The classic design of the wok has several advantages. Its rounded shape distributes heat evenly so that all the contents of the pan cook at an even rate. It lends itself easily to the constant stirring and mixing that is a part of stir-fry cooking. Because of its shape the wok is less likely to burn and is easier to clean than conventionally shaped pans.

Woks are made in iron, stainless steel, or aluminum. We strongly recommend the iron version because it distributes heat better and, thus, produces a more predictable cooking result.

Wok on ring and cover

The wok comes in a range of sizes from 10 inches (the top diameter of the pan) to 36 inches. The larger sizes are used mainly in restaurants. A 12- or 14-inch wok is the best size for general home use. Woks larger than this are awkward to use on a regular stove and are not necessary in any case, because recipes designed for home use do not require the larger size.

WHERE DO YOU BUY A WOK? Almost any large department store or reasonably sophisticated cookware shop will carry woks. Be sure to get a three-piece set that includes a ring base and a lid, in addition to the wok itself. (The purpose of the ring base is to keep the round-bottomed wok from tipping on the stove and the wok rests on this base.)

If you don't have a store in your community that sells woks, you can order them easily by mail. In an appendix to this book we list some nationwide mail-order sources for Chinese cooking equipment.

"SEASONING" YOUR NEW WOK When you buy a new iron wok you will need to "season" it, just as you would a new cast-iron skillet, to prevent food from sticking to the pan.

First, wash the new wok carefully with soap or detergent to remove the coating of oil (the oil coating is to prevent rusting). Dry the wok and place it for a couple of minutes over high heat on your stove to make sure it is thoroughly dry. Then put in two tablespoons of peanut oil (always use peanut oil in Chinese cooking when oil is called for) and slosh it around the inside surface by tilting the wok while it is on the stove burner. Continue this for a couple of minutes. Then wash the wok, using hot water and detergent and a soft sponge (no abrasive materials), and dry it thoroughly. Go through this process a second time, dry thoroughly, and your wok is seasoned and ready. With continued use your wok will acquire a better and better cooking surface and it will turn dark in color.

CLEANING THE WOK When you have cooked with your iron wok, clean it with hot water, soap or detergent, and a soft sponge. If some food has stuck to the wok, let it sit in hot water before washing to loosen the food but do not scrape the wok with a scraping tool or abrasive cloth, and do not put it in a dishwasher. This would remove part of the special coating that helps to prevent food from sticking and burning. After washing a wok make sure to dry it immediately and thoroughly, as you would a cast-iron skillet, to avoid rusting. If some rust does appear, wash it again, dry carefully, and rub on some peanut oil.

If you buy a stainless-steel or aluminum wok, you don't need to go through these seasoning or special cleaning procedures. You may prefer stainless steel or aluminum for that reason, but we recommend the iron wok for better cooking results.

SUBSTITUTE In place of a wok you can use a regular skillet, preferably cast iron.

CHINESE CLEAVER

The cleaver is a very important implement for the Chinese cook because so many Chinese recipes require sliced or chopped meats and vegetables. The Chinese cleaver is a hefty, wide-bladed knife made of an untempered steel that is very easy to keep sharp. Cleavers come in heavy-duty and medium-weight versions. The medium-weight cleaver is easier to handle, but the heavy-duty kind is better for cutting heavier meats and bones. If you are only going to get one cleaver, and that is enough for most people, get the medium-weight one.

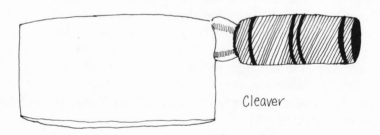

Cleaver

You can buy the cleaver (*choy doh*) at the same department store or cookware department that carries woks, or you can order by mail from the places listed under Mail-Order Sources.

CLEANING The untempered steel cleaver, like the cast-iron wok, will rust if not given proper care. Wash the cleaver by hand in hot water and soap or detergent (a dishwasher will dull the blade and harm the handle) and dry very carefully. If rust spots should occur, rub on a little peanut oil.

SUBSTITUTE You can use your heaviest-duty regular kitchen knife in place of the cleaver, but the more versatile cleaver is definitely preferred.

STEAMER

At some point as you progress in Chinese cooking skills you will probably want to acquire a bamboo steamer. The steamer is generally bought in two (or more) cooking sections plus a lid. It may be hard to find in many communities but can be ordered by mail from the companies listed under Mail-Order Sources.

You use the steamer in combination with a wok. Put two inches or so of water in the wok and place the three-part steamer right in the wok. Boiling the water in the wok circulates steam through the steamer to cook the foods that are placed in the cooking levels of the steamer.

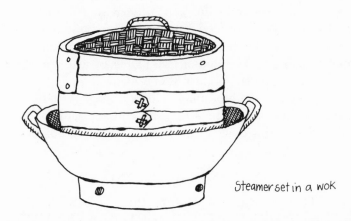

Steamer set in a wok

SUBSTITUTES There are various multipart aluminum steamers available that can be used in place of the bamboo steamer. The aluminum steamers have their own water compartment so they do not need to be used with a wok.

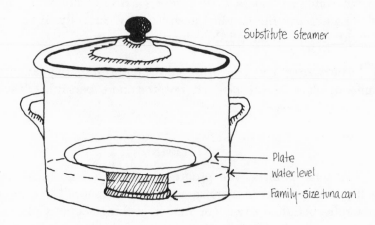

Substitute steamer

Plate
Water level
Family-size tuna can

Or more simply, you can substitute for the steamer by creating your own. Use a wide 6-quart pot, at least 10 inches in diameter, with a lid. In the pot you will need a platform to hold the food to be steamed above the level of the boiling water. This can be a high-legged metal rack if you have one, or a short, wide can (a family-size tunafish can will do) with both ends removed. Make sure the rack or can is at least two inches higher than the level of the water in the pan, otherwise you may end up with boiled, not steamed, food. Put the food to be steamed on an 8-inch metal or heat-resistant plate that rests on the rack or the tin-can platform. Then pour one or two inches of water in the pot, bring to a boil, put on the lid and steam away.

A regular double boiler will *not* work for Chinese steaming because live steam must be in contact with the food being cooked, and this does not happen in a double boiler.

CHINESE LADLE AND SPATULA

You may want to acquire the specially designed Chinese cooking ladle (*siou hok*) and spatula (*wok chan*). They will give your stir-frying a little more style and efficiency because they are specially shaped to use with a wok, but these implements are not essential at the beginning. Standard cooking spoons and spatulas can be used instead.

PREPARATION AND COOKING TECHNIQUES

Just as you will see there is nothing mysterious about the ingredients in Chinese cooking, there is nothing intimidating about their preparation and cooking techniques. They are ingenious and perfectly suited to their purposes, and quite simple to learn and to use. You will find these techniques helpful to you in much of the cooking you do; they are not reserved for the Chinese cook alone.

A great deal of the variety in Chinese cooking comes simply from the many different ways in which the same ingredients can be cut up and combined in different recipes. There is one important thing to remember, though. To produce a pleasing appearance for the eye and a consistent texture for the palate, the Chinese usually use the same cutting style for all the major ingredients in any given recipe. If the recipe calls for the meat to be diced, the vegetables to be combined with it will be diced, too, in the same size cubes. If the meat is to be in strips, the vegetables will be in strips too. Variety comes in the fact that another recipe will use the same or similar ingredients in a chopped form; another time they will be cut in larger pieces; still another time they will be shredded.

You will get a lot of practice in Chinese cooking in chopping, slicing, mincing, cubing, and shredding. For this the all-purpose cleaver is a great aid.

USING THE CLEAVER

First, be sure the blade is sharp. A dull cleaver, like a dull knife, is not only less efficient but also a more dangerous instrument than a sharp one. You can sharpen your cleaver in the same way you sharpen your knives.

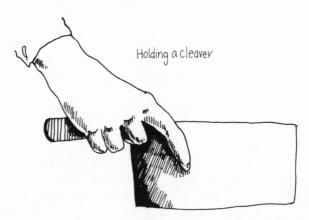

Holding a cleaver

When cutting with a cleaver, as with a knife, first, of course, be careful. Don't attempt to get fancy with it until, and unless, you are an expert. Don't go too fast or lift the blade too high. Keep the fingers of the hand that is holding the food tucked under so that the knuckles, not the fingertips, are resting against the flat side of the cleaver. Hold the cleaver with your index finger along the top of the blade to steady it. Do not lift the cleaver blade above the level of the knuckles. Get used to keeping your knuckles in contact with the side of the cleaver and your fingers tucked under for safety's sake. If the cleaver is sharp, the cutting can be done with an easy, unforced motion that does not require a lot of pressure.

Here are the five basic cutting styles used in Chinese cooking:

SLICING In regular slicing, used for all meats and most vegetables, cut thin, vertical slices 1½ inches square and ⅛ inch or so thick. Meat should always be sliced against the grain to make it more tender and to show a better texture.

Some recipes will call for angled slicing. For this, rather than slicing vertically, cut at a 45° angle away from you. Meat will slice better if it is slightly frozen.

MINCING Slice the meat or vegetable as described above, then put both hands on top of the cleaver and chop with quick, short, vertical strokes until the pieces are very small.

CUTTING IN CUBES Cut the meat or vegetables first lengthwise in strips 1 inch wide, then cut the strips in the other direction to produce cubes of approximately 1 inch.

DICING Use the same system as for cutting 1-inch cubes but make the pieces ¼-inch to ½-inch sizes as called for in the recipe.

SHREDDING First slice the meat or vegetable about ⅛ inch thick as indicated in Slicing (above) and then cut the slices lengthwise into thin shreds about ⅛ inch wide.

There is nothing complicated about any of this. You may be slow at first, and you should certainly be cautious, but you will develop speed and assurance as you get used to using the cleaver.

COOKING METHODS

Chinese cooking techniques are even simpler to learn; it generally takes less time for the preparation of a meal than for the advance chopping and slicing. The Chinese use many different cooking methods, but the four main ones, the ones we will concentrate on in this book, are stir-frying, oven-roasting, steaming, and deep (fat) frying. The Chinese (Cantonese) terms for these four methods are *chow, shu, jing,* and *jow.*

STIR-FRYING The food is cooked for a short time over high heat in a wok or frying pan. You are introduced to stir-frying in Menu Lesson 1.

OVEN-ROASTING Meats are cooked in the oven with a special method described in Menu Lesson 2.

DEEP FRYING The food is cooked in hot peanut oil in a saucepan, wok, or electric frying pan, as described in Menu Lesson 3.

STEAMING The food is cooked directly over steam in a wok-steamer combination or in a substitute steamer described earlier. The steaming technique is explained in Menu Lesson 4.

SERVING
AND EATING
A CHINESE DINNER

In China food is usually served in either of two ways: family style, in which all the food dishes are placed on the table at one time; or banquet style, in which the dishes are brought out individually.

A true Chinese banquet is an extravagant dinner consisting of many different courses, beginning with a platter of cold dishes, proceeding to lighter stir-fried dishes of seafood and chicken, then perhaps to a light soup and some sweets to clear the palate before continuing with heavier meat dishes. Finally the dinner ends with a hearty soup. Warmed rice wine is served in tiny cups throughout the banquet.

You will want to experience a full-fledged banquet at a good Chinese restaurant, but in this book we generally suggest that you serve your own Chinese meals family style. When soup or

19

dessert is included in a meal, we have followed the Western style of serving soup first and dessert last. The Chinese typically serve soup along with the other courses, and dessert generally not at all, although a sweet dish might be incorporated some-where in the meal.

SETTING THE TABLE

The Chinese use special table dishes, which you have un-doubtedly seen. These include the graceful rice bowl or soup bowl (they are interchangeable), the Chinese teacup (it is small and has no handle), the porcelain spoon (it doesn't conduct heat), and, of course, chopsticks. You do not need to use these special Chinese dishes but it's more fun if you do.

To serve one of the Chinese dinners described in this book family style, set your table as follows:

In the center of each place setting there should be a dinner plate with a smaller service plate set on it. If soup is to be served, a soup bowl with a porcelain spoon resting in it should be placed on top of the service plate. A rice bowl is put at the upper left and chopsticks just to the right of the plate. Place the wineglass and/or teacup on the upper right above the chopsticks.

Table setting with a teapot

If soup is on the menu, serve it from a large tureen or casserole into the individual bowls at each place setting. When the soup is finished remove the bowls, leaving behind the smaller service plate. This plate will be used for a first course, such as dumplings, egg rolls, shrimp toast, etc. Next, remove the smaller service plate, leaving the dinner plate. The rest of the food will be placed in the center of the table in serving bowls. Guests will help themselves. Rice is served in individual bowls throughout the dinner. Dessert will be served at the end of the meal according to Western custom.

CHOPSTICKS

Chopsticks are not really hard to learn to use. Hold one chopstick in a stationary position with its upper end resting at the base of your thumb and forefinger and the lower end held

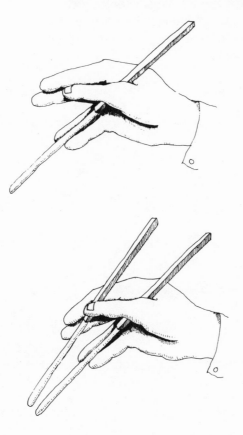

firmly with the tips of your little finger and ring finger. The other chopstick is held with the tips of your thumb, index finger, and middle finger. It is moved in a pincer movement so that food can be grasped by bringing together the tips of the pincering upper chopstick and the stationary lower chopstick. You can make sure the ends of the two chopsticks are evenly lined up by tapping them lightly on your plate. Once you have had a little practice with them you will find chopsticks surprisingly efficient eating instruments.

BEVERAGES

What do you drink with a Chinese meal? You may want to follow the common practice in Chinese restaurants here and serve tea continually during the meal, although the Chinese would ordinarily drink tea only after the meal. During the meal in China soups are served as beverage and, on special occasions, rice wine. Good rice wine is not easy to find here, so, if you wish, you can substitute beer or a dry white table wine.

INGREDIENTS

Many of the ingredients you will use in Chinese recipes are foods you are already completely familiar with: standard cuts of beef and pork, chicken, duckling, shrimp, fish, clams, lobster, crabmeat, string beans, carrots, broccoli, eggplant, scallions, peppers, peanuts and cashews, eggs, rice, pineapple, cherries, honey, and ice cream.

Then there are a number of special Chinese vegetables and fruits that you will use, including various mushrooms, bamboo shoots, snow peas, water chestnuts, bean sprouts, Chinese cabbage, baby corn, cellophane noodles, egg roll wrappers, winter and summer melons, lichee nuts, and kumquats.

And there are the great Chinese flavorings and sauces, such as ginger, bean paste, bean curd, bean sauce, oyster sauce, plum sauce, and, of course, soy sauce. Many of these are available in cans and some can be stored indefinitely.

Many Western cooks are reluctant to try Chinese cooking because they assume the ingredients they will need are too difficult to find, and in any case too exotic to serve to most people. You will see that this is just not so.

Following is a list of the ingredients most used in Chinese cooking. The list does not include regular cuts of meats and standard vegetables and fruits because everyone knows these. At the other end of the spectrum the list also leaves out some of the rarer Chinese specialties, but it does cover all the Chinese ingredients that you will need for recipes in this book and for most other Chinese recipes.

The ingredients list tells you what the food is like, where it comes from, how it is most frequently used, where to buy it, how to store it, how to prepare it for use, and what, if anything, can be substituted if it is not readily available.

We suggest you read through this list once to get a general understanding of what is included. Then refer back to it when you are planning each meal to look up the specific information on any ingredient that is new to you in a recipe.

AGAR-AGAR is a dried seaweed usually packaged in long, thin strips to be used in salads. It has very little flavor of its own but absorbs the flavors of the dressing and adds a slightly chewy texture to the salad. Agar-agar also comes in powdered or compressed forms used to make gelatin. It can be purchased in Chinese food stores or by mail. It must be soaked before using.

To Soak: For use in salads, soak agar-agar strips in *cold* water for two hours. Change the water after the first hour. After soaking, rinse and cut into 2-inch sections. If agar-agar is to be used for gelatin, soak in *hot* water until dissolved and then strain.

To Store: Keep agar-agar in a tied plastic bag on the pantry shelf. It will keep indefinitely.

Substitution: None for the strips to be used in salads. Unflavored gelatin can be substituted if the agar-agar is to be made into gelatin.

ANISE, STAR. See *Star Anise*.

BABY EARS OF CORN are miniature ears of corn on the cob sold in cans in Chinese markets. They are also available imported from France in gourmet food stores or by mail. They are already cooked and require only heating.

To Store: Once the can has been opened cover the remaining ears with cold water and store in a covered container in the refrigerator. If you change the water every other day they should last two weeks.

BAMBOO SHOOTS are the actual growing shoots of the Oriental bamboo. They are added to various dishes to give a crunchy texture. They may be purchased fresh in a Chinese grocery or are widely available in cans. The canned shoots come packed in water or brine. We prefer those packed in water. Those packed in brine are too salty. Rinse the canned bamboo shoots several times in fresh water before cooking or, if there is time, soak them in ice water in the refrigerator for several hours. The fresh water will remove the "tinny" taste of the can. Bamboo shoots are available in most supermarkets now, but if you cannot find them, order by mail.

To Store: Cover with cold water and store in a covered container in the refrigerator. If you change the water every other day they should last two weeks.

Substitution: Carrots.

BEAN CURD is made from soybeans that have been puréed and then boiled to remove the strong soybean flavor. A coagulant is then added that curdles the liquid. It is a staple of the Oriental diet and is a rich source of protein. Bean curd comes in many forms, depending upon its preparation—fresh, dried, pressed, fried, and fermented. It is often added to vegetable and meat dishes or soup for greater nutritive value. You may add it to any of the stir-fried meat or vegetable dishes in this book for additional protein and interesting texture.

FRESH BEAN CURD has the texture and appearance of custard and a mild, delicate taste. It is cut into small 3-inch squares and sold in Chinese markets. It is also available in cans imported from Japan and called *tofu*. There is also an instant *tofu* prepared by the Japanese that can be made at home and substituted for the fresh. These are generally available in health food stores or by mail.

To Store: Fresh bean curd should be kept in fresh water in a container in the refrigerator. If the water is changed every other day the bean curd should keep about one week.

FRIED BEAN CURD comes in 2-inch cubes. The curds have been deep fried so they are crusty outside and still soft inside. They are generally eaten stuffed with a filling.

To Store: Fried bean curd will keep in the refrigerator two or three days or up to three months in the freezer.

DRIED BEAN CURD comes in very thin fragile strips. It is made from the skin that forms on the surface when the soybean liquid is boiled. It is soaked first, then added to stir-fried dishes or soups.

To Soak: Cover with hot water and set aside for 30 minutes.

To Store: It can be kept in a tied plastic bag several months on the pantry shelf.

PRESSED BEAN CURD has had much of the liquid pressed from it so it is quite solid. It is sold in 3-inch squares, either white or brown. The white is plain; the brown has been cooked in soy sauce and spices.

To Store: Cover with salted water and refrigerate. It should last two to three weeks.

Substitution for Bean Curd: None.

BEAN SAUCE. See *Brown Bean Sauce*.

BEAN SPROUTS are crisp, white shoots grown from soybeans or mung beans. Mung bean sprouts are more commonly used in this country; they are smaller and more tender. Bean sprouts can be grown at home (see page 47), or purchased fresh in a Chinese grocery or in cans in most supermarkets. The canned sprouts lack the crispness and flavor of fresh sprouts, but they can be improved by being soaked in ice water for a few hours before they are cooked.

To Store: Cover with cold water and store in a covered container in the refrigerator. If you change the water every other day they should last one week.

Substitution: Shredded iceberg lettuce.

BIRD'S NEST is a special gelatinlike material produced by Asian swallows in the creation of their nests. It is used in the famed banquet delicacy, Bird's Nest Soup. We do not offer a recipe for the soup because it is rarely made at home, but we thought you would like to know what it is.

BLACK BEANS, FERMENTED, are small, black soybeans the size of peas that have been preserved in salt. They have a strong, pungent flavor. They are available in jars or in plastic bags in Chinese groceries or by mail. They must be soaked before using.
To Soak: Cover with cold water and set aside for 15 minutes. Drain before using.
To Store: Place in an airtight covered jar in the refrigerator. They will keep indefinitely.
Substitution: Salt to taste.

BOK CHOY. See *Cabbage, Chinese.*

BROCCOLI, CHINESE, is a dark-green vegetable more leafy than the broccoli available in markets here. It grows in stalks about 12 inches long and is very similar in flavor to Western broccoli.
To Store: It should be kept in the vegetable bin of your refrigerator; it will keep up to one week.
Substitution: Broccoli.

BROWN BEAN SAUCE is made from fermented soybeans and salt. The beans are either ground or whole. The sauce is available in jars or cans in Chinese groceries or by mail. It is often cooked with fish or chicken dishes to impart a full-bodied, salty flavor.
To Store: When a can is opened transfer the remaining sauce to a covered container and refrigerate. It will keep indefinitely.
Substitution: A beef extract, such as Bovril, to taste.

CABBAGE, CELERY, (also called Celery Lettuce) is a vegetable about 12 inches long with tightly packed stalks and yellow-green curly tops. It is sold by the pound and is available in most greengrocers. The entire plant is cooked and eaten.

To Store: It should keep about one week in the vegetable bin of your refrigerator.

Substitution: Savoy cabbage, celery, or spinach.

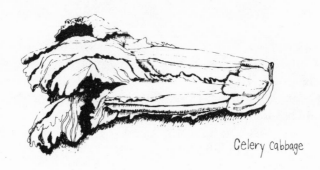

Celery Cabbage

CABBAGE, CHINESE, (also called *Bok Choy*) is a very popular fresh vegetable with milky white stalks about 12 inches long and dark green leaves. It is sold by the bunch in Chinese groceries. The entire plant is cooked and eaten. Sometimes you will see the cabbage in the market topped with delicate yellow flowers that can also be eaten.

To Store: It should keep about one week in the vegetable bin of your refrigerator.

Substitution: Celery cabbage or Savoy cabbage.

CASHEW NUTS are sold raw, blanched, and shelled by the pound in Chinese groceries or by mail. They must be roasted before using them.

To Roast: Heat 2 tablespoons of oil in a skillet and sauté the nuts until they are golden brown.

To Store: Keep in a covered jar or a tied plastic bag on the pantry shelf. They will keep for a couple of months but will eventually turn rancid.

Substitution: Dry roasted cashews, but use less salt than the recipe calls for.

CELERY CABBAGE. See *Cabbage, Celery*.

CELERY LETTUCE. See *Cabbage, Celery.*

CELLOPHANE NOODLES. See *Noodles, Cellophane.*

CHICKEN BROTH is a concentrated stock made from chicken. The canned variety is simpler to use than the cubes and so it is recommended in the recipes in this book. You can, however, make your own using chicken bones, gizzards, and necks cooked with salt and pepper. If you use the canned broth make sure you purchase the broth made with no flavorings added other than salt.
Substitution: Although the broth makes a much richer sauce, water can be substituted.

CHILI PASTE WITH GARLIC is sold in jars in Chinese food stores or by mail. This sauce is very hot and should be used sparingly. It is a combination of chili peppers, garlic, and spices and is used to season Szechuan dishes.
To Store: After opening the jar store in the refrigerator. It will keep for several months.
Substitution: Tabasco sauce to taste.

CHILI PEPPERS, DRIED, are whole, dried red peppers, 1 to 2 inches in length, and are extremely hot. They are sold in small plastic bags or in bulk by weight. They are used extensively in Szechuan cooking and are available in Chinese or Italian groceries or by mail. Always wash your hands carefully with soap and water after handling them so that the oily residue doesn't irritate. When using these peppers in a recipe cut them in half and knock out some of the seeds. This will make the peppers less hot. Remove peppers before serving.
To Store: Keep in a tied plastic bag or an airtight container on the pantry shelf. They will lose some of their "hotness" after a few months.
Substitution: Red pepper flakes (¼ teaspoon per whole pepper) or Tabasco sauce to taste.

CHINESE BROCCOLI. See *Broccoli, Chinese.*

CLOUD EAR. See *Mushrooms, Cloud Ear.*

CORIANDER (also called Chinese Parsley) is the flat-leaf parsley
available in most supermarkets. It has more flavor than regular parsley and is often used as a garnish on Chinese dishes.
Coriander is called *cilantro* in an Italian market and *culantro*
in a Spanish market.
To Store: Place cut stem ends in a glass of water and refrigerate. It will keep about one week.
Substitution: Parsley.

CORNSTARCH is a powder or flour made from corn that is used to
thicken sauces and soups, in marinades, and for dredging
before frying. Cornstarch seals in the juices in cooking meat,
seafood, or poultry. It is always dissolved in a small amount
of cold water before being added as a thickener to a sauce
or soup. Remember to stir the dissolved cornstarch in the
water before adding it to a dish because it will have settled.
Do not add the dissolved cornstarch thickener to a dish until
just before serving or it will become "gluey."
Substitution: Do not substitute flour. It will make your sauce
too heavy. Cornstarch is available in all markets.

DRIED CHINESE MUSHROOMS. See *Mushrooms, Dried Chinese.*

DRIED SHRIMP. See *Shrimp, Dried.*

DUMPLING SKINS OR WRAPPERS are circles of dough about 3 inches
in diameter made from eggs, flour, and water that are used
for both fried and steamed dumplings. They can be purchased in a Chinese food market, or by mail in 1-pound
packages, or they can be made at home (see recipe).
To Store: Wrap carefully in airtight plastic bags and freeze
until needed.

EGG ROLL SKINS OR WRAPPERS (WON TON SKINS OR WRAPPERS) are
sheets of dough about 8 inches square made from eggs, flour,
and water that are used to wrap egg rolls. They can be purchased in a Chinese food market, or by mail in 1-pound

packages, or they can be made at home (see recipe). Won ton skins are made from the same dough but cut into smaller squares, about 3 inches.

To Store: Wrap carefully in airtight plastic bags and freeze until needed.

FERMENTED BLACK BEANS. See *Black Beans, Fermented.*

FIVE-SPICE POWDER is a premixed combination of various ground spices and seasonings, principally anise, cloves, Szechuan pepper, fennel, and cinnamon. It is sold in Chinese food stores and by mail.

To Store: Keep tightly covered in a jar on your spice shelf.

Substitution: Allspice.

FLANK STEAK is the beef recommended in the stir-fried dishes in this book. When cut and marinated according to directions it is tender and flavorful. There is no bone and little fat, so flank steak is a more economical cut of beef.

To Store: Cut the flank steak lengthwise into three long strips, wrap in foil, and freeze. When you are ready to use the meat, thaw slightly and cut diagonally into ¼-inch slices. Semifrozen meat is much easier to slice thin.

Substitution: Sirloin or beef tenderloin.

GARLIC is a common seasoning vegetable in Chinese cooking. Try to buy fresh, plump garlic bulbs. The recipes in this book call for teaspoon measurements. Keep in mind that 2 average-size garlic cloves equal 1 teaspoon minced garlic.

To Store: Keep in a covered jar on the pantry shelf.

GINGER ROOT is a very common Chinese seasoning ingredient that looks like a twisted root. It is brown on the outside and yellow-white inside and has a sharp, pungent taste. Ginger root can be purchased in Chinese food stores, some specialty food shops, and by mail. To use, cut off a piece of the root, wash it (it is not necessary to peel it), and use as the recipe directs.

Ginger root

To Store: The whole ginger root can be kept for two to three weeks in a plastic bag or a tightly covered jar in the refrigerator. You can keep peeled ginger indefinitely in the refrigerator in a jar filled with dry sherry or you may freeze it. If it is to be frozen, cut the root up into 1-inch segments and freeze them in separate plastic bags so you don't have to defrost the whole root when you need only part of it.

NOTE: It is best to slice ginger root while it is still partially frozen. It will not lose as much of its juice.

Substitution: Regular powdered ginger doesn't have the same sharp flavor as fresh ginger and is therefore not a suitable substitute. However, the Dutch have a ground ginger under the brand name Conimex that is a good substitute. Look for it in specialty food stores to have on hand in case you should run out of the fresh ginger.

GINKGO NUT is a small round "nut" (actually it is a pit) with white meat. It is used in vegetable dishes and soups. In this book it is used in the recipe for Buddha's Delight. The "nuts" are sold dried or in cans in Chinese food stores or by mail. Dried ginkgo nuts must be shelled and blanched before using them.
To Blanch: Pour boiling water over the shelled nuts and set aside for 15 minutes. Drain and peel off the pink skin.
To Store: Keep in an airtight plastic bag on the pantry shelf.
Substitution: Blanched almonds.

GLUTINOUS RICE. See *Rice, Glutinous*.

GROUND BEAN SAUCE. See *Brown Bean Sauce*.

HAM, CHINESE, is used as a flavoring and meat accent in various salad, soup, and fried rice dishes and other recipes. Smith-

field ham most closely approximates Chinese ham.
Substitution: Any smoked ham.

HOISIN SAUCE is a sweet, yet somewhat spicy, thick, brown-colored
sauce made from soybeans combined with various seasonings.
Used in quite a number of Chinese recipes, it can be purchased in tins in Chinese food stores, some specialty food
shops, or by mail.
To Store: When the can is opened transfer the remaining
sauce to a covered jar. It will keep indefinitely in the
refrigerator.
Substitution: None.

HOT PEPPER OIL is a red-colored oil flavored with hot peppers and
is available in small bottles in Chinese food stores or by
mail. It is used in dipping sauces for dumplings. We use it
with the recipe for Steamed Beef Dumplings. It is also placed
on the table with rice vinegar as a seasoning to be used with
noodles or dumplings.
To Store: It will keep indefinitely on the pantry shelf.
Substitution: You can make it at home by heating ½ cup
of peanut oil to 375° and frying 3 dried red chili peppers
until they turn black. Remove the peppers and store the oil
in a small covered jar.

LICHEE FRUIT is a small, red, sweet-tasting fruit that has the shape
of a large berry. It is used as a sweet snack and in some
recipes. It is sold fresh in the spring in Chinese markets,
otherwise it is available in cans in Chinese food stores or by
mail.
To Store: Once a can has been opened store the remaining
lichees in their syrup in a covered jar in the refrigerator.

LICHEE NUTS are dried lichees with a nutty taste that are usually
eaten as a treat between meals much as raisins would be.
They are sold in cellophane bags or boxes and are available
in Chinese food stores or by mail.
To Store: Place in a tied plastic bag on the pantry shelf.
They will keep indefinitely.

LONGAN (also called Dragon Eye) is a delicately flavored fruit that is the size of a cherry. It is used as a sweet snack and in some sweet soup recipes. Longans can be purchased in cans in Chinese food stores or by mail.
To Store: Once the can has been opened, store the remaining longans in their syrup in a covered jar in the refrigerator.

LOQUAT is a yellow-colored fruit that looks and tastes somewhat like an apricot. It is used as a sweet snack and in some recipes. It can be purchased in cans in Chinese food stores and by mail.
To Store: Once the can has been opened store the remaining loquats in their syrup in a covered jar in the refrigerator.

LOTUS ROOT is a root of the lotus plant or water lily and resembles a sweet potato. It is used as a vegetable and sometimes in sweet dishes. It is available in Chinese food stores or by mail. It is sometimes sold fresh but more often dried or in cans. Dried lotus root must be soaked before cooking.
To Soak: Place in a bowl with hot water to cover for about 30 minutes.
To Store: Fresh lotus root can be kept in the refrigerator for about three weeks. Dried lotus root will keep in tied plastic bags on the pantry shelf indefinitely.
Substitution: None.

Lotus root

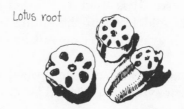

MONOSODIUM GLUTAMATE (MSG) is a flavoring powder that is used by some Chinese cooks and restaurants to enhance the flavor of meat and vegetable dishes. If it is used it should be in small amounts. Many people prefer not to use monosodium glutamate at all, feeling that chemical flavor enhancers are not necessary when good ingredients are used. There is also an unresolved controversy about the health consequences of using substantial amounts of monosodium glutamate. We do not use MSG in the recipes in this book.

MUSHROOMS, CANNED, are the same white button mushrooms used by cooks here. They are whole, sliced, or diced and packed in water.
Substitution: Fresh white mushrooms or American canned mushrooms.

MUSHROOMS, CLOUD EARS OR TREE EARS, are small dried mushrooms or fungi that are brown-black in color and irregularly shaped. They must be soaked before using in a recipe. When soaked they expand to several times the original size and are slightly rubbery in texture. Cloud ears are often used in combination with tiger lily buds in a recipe. They are available in Chinese food stores or by mail.
To Soak: Rinse well in cold water to remove any sand, then soak in warm water for 30 minutes. Rinse again in cold water and trim off any hard stems.
To Store: Wrap in an airtight plastic bag and store on the pantry shelf. They will keep indefinitely.
Substitution: None.

MUSHROOMS, DRIED CHINESE, are imported from China or Japan and are sold in Chinese food stores or by mail. They are brown in color with flat caps about 1 to 2 inches across. They are used widely in Chinese cooking. Dried Chinese mushrooms must be soaked before adding them to a recipe.
To Soak: Rinse in cold water to remove any sand and soak

Dried mushrooms

in warm water for 30 minutes. Remove the tough stem section and discard.

To Store: Dried mushrooms will keep indefinitely on the pantry shelf in a covered jar or in an airtight plastic bag. Tuck a peeled clove of garlic in to prevent the mushrooms from becoming "webby."

Substitution: Dried black mushrooms from Europe. However, use fewer than the Chinese recipe calls for because they are stronger in flavor.

MUSHROOMS, STRAW, are a very delicate variety of mushroom with a conical cap. They are available in cans or dried from Chinese food stores or by mail. The dried mushrooms must be soaked before using them.

To Soak: Rinse in cold water to remove any sand and soak in warm water for 15 minutes.

To Store: Wrap in an airtight plastic bag and store on the pantry shelf. They will keep indefinitely.

Substitution: Canned button mushroom caps.

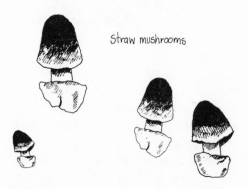

Straw mushrooms

NOODLES, CELLOPHANE, are very thin noodles made from ground mung beans. (The very same beans used to grow bean sprouts.) Cellophane noodles have very little flavor of their own but absorb the flavors of the ingredients in the dish. They come in 2-ounce packets and are sold in Chinese food stores or by mail. The noodles must be soaked in hot water at the time they are used in a recipe. When warm they are clear and have the appearance of cellophane, hence the name.

To Soak: Place noodles in a large bowl and pour boiling water over to cover. Set aside for 15 minutes. Drain, then rinse in cold water.

To Store: Cellophane noodles will keep in tied plastic bags on the pantry shelf indefinitely.

Substitution: Very thin spaghetti or egg noodles.

NOODLES, EGG, are made from flour and eggs. Egg noodles can be bought fresh from the refrigerated cabinets in Chinese food stores (they are soft), or dried from Chinese food stores, or by mail.

To Store: Egg noodles will keep two to three weeks in the refrigerator if fresh, or indefinitely on the pantry shelf if dried.

Substitution: Regular thin, dried egg noodles found in any store.

NOODLES, RICE, (also called Rice Sticks) are delicate, very thin noodles made from rice flour. They are used in soups and many other dishes. If they are to be used in a stir-fried recipe they should be soaked first. Rice noodles are available in cellophane bags in Chinese food stores or by mail.

To Soak: Place noodles in a large bowl and pour boiling water over to cover. Set aside for 30 minutes. Drain, then rinse in cold water.

To Store: Rice noodles will keep in a tied plastic bag on the pantry shelf indefinitely.

Substitution: Vermicelli.

OYSTER SAUCE is a thick, brown, salty, richly flavored seasoning made from ground oysters and soy sauce. It is used in various stir-fried meat recipes and sometimes as a seasoning for meats at the table. Oyster sauce is sold in bottles in Chinese food stores or by mail.

To Store: Oyster sauce can be kept in its original bottle indefinitely in the refrigerator.

Substitution: None.

PEA PODS. See *Snow Peas*.

PEANUTS are sold raw, blanched, and shelled by the pound in
Chinese groceries or by mail. They must be roasted before
using them.
To Roast: Heat 2 tablespoons of oil in a skillet and sauté the
nuts until they are golden brown.
To Store: Keep in a covered jar or a tied plastic bag on the
pantry shelf. They will keep for a couple of months but will
eventually turn rancid.
Substitution: Dry roasted peanuts, but use less salt than the
recipe calls for.

PEANUT OIL is used extensively as the preferred cooking oil for
both deep-fat frying and stir-frying. It is sold in bottles and
tins at most food stores. It does not absorb from or impart
flavors to the food being cooked, it does not burn at high
temperatures, and it can be reused. Peanut oil that has been
used for deep-fat frying can be reused up to four times or
until it becomes very dark in color.
To Store: Peanut oil can be kept indefinitely in a covered
glass container at room temperature. Strain out any large
particles of food before storing. It does not need to be refrigerated.
Substitution: Corn oil or vegetable oil.

PEPPERS, DRIED CHILI. See *Chili Peppers, Dried.*

PEPPER, SZECHUAN, is a spicy, hot, aromatic pepper that looks like
a regular black peppercorn but is dark red-brown in color.
Substitution: Black peppercorns.

PINE NUTS come from the pine tree. They are sold by weight,
blanched and shelled, in Chinese food stores, Italian food
stores, or by mail. The Italian name is *pignoli*. They have
a softer texture than the peanut and are about half the size.
To Store: They will keep in a tied plastic bag on the pantry
shelf for a couple of months. However, they will eventually
turn rancid.
Substitution: Blanched, slivered almonds.

PORK is the most common meat served in China. It is so common-place, in fact, that it is rarely served at a banquet where only special dishes are offered. When buying pork look for meat that is lean with good, pink color. It can be sliced, shredded, cut in cubes, or ground. Each individual recipe will give you cutting instructions. Remember always to be certain the pork is fully cooked. The cooking instructions in this book give added time for cooking pork. If you should substitute pork for poultry or beef in any of the recipes add the extra cooking time.

RICE, LONG-GRAIN, is the standard rice used in southern Chinese cooking. It is fluffier and less starchy than short-grain rice. Long-grain rice is cooked with more water (1¾ cups water per cup of raw rice) and so it yields more cooked rice. We have suggested using it in the menus in this book. Its American counterpart is sold in all food markets.

RICE, SHORT-GRAIN (OVAL GRAIN), has shorter, thicker grains and is also sold in all food markets. It requires less water for cooking and has a softer, stickier consistency than long-grain rice when cooked. If you prefer short-grain rice you may use it instead of the long grain. For each cup of raw rice use 1½ cups water, then follow cooking directions for boiled rice in Menu Lesson 1.

RICE, GLUTINOUS, (also called Sweet Rice) has grains that are even shorter and thicker than standard short-grain rice. The grains stick together in clumps when cooked and its taste is sweeter than other rice. In this book it is used in the recipe for Pearl Balls. Glutinous rice is sold in Chinese food stores or by mail. *To Soak*: Glutinous rice should be soaked in cold water for 30 minutes before cooking. If it is to be used for a coating or a stuffing it should be soaked in cold water for at least 2 hours.
To Store: Store in a dry place just as you would other rice.
Substitution: None.

RICE NOODLES. See *Noodles, Rice*.

RICE STICKS. See *Noodles, Rice*.

RICE VINEGAR is used as a flavoring in various dishes and comes in black or white color. The black vinegar is used as a condiment at the table. The recipes in this book call for white rice vinegar. The Japanese brand Kikkoman is a good-quality white rice vinegar that is generally available in supermarkets.
To Store: Rice vinegar will keep indefinitely in the refrigerator.
Substitution: White cider vinegar.

RICE WINE: The Chinese have a variety of wines made from different grains, but the best known is a dry rice wine called *Shao Hsing*. The wine is served warm in small cups like sake in Japan. Good Chinese rice wine is not generally available here so you will have to substitute.
Substitution: A dry cocktail sherry can be used for cooking. For a dinner wine, Japanese sake is a good substitute for a special occasion, or, if you prefer, you can use an American or European dry white table wine.

SAUSAGE, CHINESE, is a sweet, tasty pork sausage that can be used in a number of different steamed or stir-fried dishes. It is sold in links by weight in Chinese food stores or by mail.
To Store: Wrap well and refrigerate. It will keep up to three months.
Substitution: None.

SCALLION is a kind of onion. Scallions are sold by the bunch in greengrocers. In Chinese dishes the entire scallion is used. The green tops are often used as a garnish in soups or meat and vegetable dishes.
To Store: Scallions will keep up to a week in the vegetable bin of the refrigerator.
Substitution: Onions.

SESAME OIL is a strongly flavored seasoning with a nutlike taste that is made from roasted sesame seeds. It is not used as a cooking oil but is used instead in small quantities as a special flavoring in a variety of dishes. It is often sprinkled over Szechuan foods, although we mention in the recipes that its use is optional. It is sold in Chinese food stores, some specialized food shops, or by mail.

NOTE: Some health food stores carry another type of sesame oil made by a different process that is bland and pale in color. This, however, does not have the flavor and aroma of the highly concentrated Chinese sesame oil and should not be used in Chinese recipes.

To Store: Sesame oil keeps indefinitely in its bottle in the refrigerator.

Substitution: None.

SESAME PASTE is made from sesame seeds. It looks and tastes somewhat like peanut butter and is used in certain sauces and dressings. It can be found in Chinese food stores, by mail, and in some health food departments.

To Store: Sesame paste keeps for months in a covered jar in the refrigerator.

Substitution: Add a little sesame oil to peanut butter.

SESAME SEEDS are tiny flat seeds (both black and white) that are used as a garnish and flavoring in cold dishes, cakes, and other sweets. They can be purchased by the ounce in Chinese, Middle Eastern, and Italian markets.

To Store: Wrap in an airtight plastic bag and keep in the refrigerator. They should keep about three months but will eventually turn rancid.

Substitution: None.

SHARK'S FIN is cartilage taken from a shark's fin. It is used in the great banquet delicacy, Shark's Fin Soup. The soup is rarely made at home so we do not include a recipe. However, we thought you would be interested to know about it.

SHERRY, DRY. See *Rice Wine*.

SHRIMP, DRIED, are tiny shelled, dried shrimp that are preserved in salt, so they have quite a salty taste. They are used in the recipe for Spicy Green Beans. They are sold dry by weight in Chinese food stores or by mail. They must be soaked before adding to a recipe.

To Soak: Rinse the shrimp in cold water, then cover with warm water and set aside for 30 minutes. Rinse again in cold water and drain.

To Store: Store dried shrimp (before soaking) at room temperature in a covered container or a tied plastic bag.

Substitution: You can use regular shrimp (shelled and cooked) if dried shrimp aren't available. You would, of course, use a smaller quantity of the regular-size shrimp than of the tiny dried shrimp.

SNOW PEAS (also called Pea Pods) are tender young peas that are cooked and eaten in the pod. Cooked for the very short time called for in stir-fried recipes, snow peas add a crisp taste, a delicate flavor, and a bright green color to many dishes. Snow peas are sold fresh in Chinese food stores and some specialty food shops. Frozen snow peas are now available in many supermarkets and you can even grow your own. To prepare fresh snow peas for cooking, break off the stem and discard the string that goes along the spine of the pod. This is not necessary for frozen snow peas.

To Store: Store fresh snow peas in a plastic bag in the refrigerator. They can be stored for up to a week but they are best used the day you buy them.

Substitution: You can use regular frozen green peas or fresh peas (but don't use the pods in this case because the pods of regular peas are too tough).

SOY SAUCE is a rich, salty brown liquid made by fermenting soy beans with salt and wheat. Soy sauce is the basic seasoning used in Chinese cooking. It gives color, flavor, and body to a wide variety of sauces for meat and vegetable dishes. It is also used in soups, marinades, and dips and as a seasoning at the table. The Chinese make both light and dark soy sauces. If you have both, the light is used when a more delicate flavor and little color is wanted, as in clear soup. The dark soy sauce would be used with meat dishes and in other recipes in which a heartier flavor and darker color are preferred. If it is not convenient for you to have both light and dark soy sauce, you can instead use Japanese soy sauce, which falls between the light and dark Chinese soy sauce in color and flavor. A good-quality Japanese soy sauce that is widely available in supermarkets is the Kikkoman brand. Chinese and Japanese soy sauces are generally preferred by Chinese cooks over most American soy sauces, which are made by a different process and tend to be somewhat bitter and more salty.

To Store: Soy sauce can be kept indefinitely at room temperature in its original bottle.

Substitution: In a pinch, although this is not recommended, you can use salt for seasoning purposes in place of soy sauce —use ½ teaspoon of salt in place of 1 tablespoon of soy sauce.

SPRING ROLL SKINS OR WRAPPERS are generally bought ready-made in either round or square shapes in packages of 10 or 15. They are available in Chinese food stores or by mail. They are very, very thin and resemble the Mandarin Pancakes used in Peking Duck and Mu Shu Pork. They are thinner and lighter than egg roll skins. (See recipe.)

To Store: Wrap carefully in airtight plastic bags and freeze.

STAR ANISE is a licorice-flavored spice used to flavor some meat and poultry dishes. The star anise has the shape of eight-pointed stars. It is sold dry by the ounce in Chinese food stores or by mail.

To Store: Star anise can be stored indefinitely on the pantry shelf in a tied plastic bag or a covered jar.

Substitution: Two or three drops of anise extract found in most drugstores.

Star anise

STRAW MUSHROOMS. See *Mushrooms, Straw*.

SWEET RICE. See *Rice, Glutinous*.

SZECHUAN PEPPER. See *Pepper, Szechuan*.

THOUSAND-YEAR EGGS are raw chicken or duck eggs that have been coated with a mixture of lime, ashes, and salt and buried in the ground for about three months. The coating and the aging in the ground turn the egg dark in color throughout and solidify the white and yolk to resemble an antique hard-boiled egg. The eggs are usually eaten uncooked as an appetizer or as a banquet specialty. Thousand-year eggs can be bought at Chinese food stores. To use them as an appetizer, clean off the "mud" coating thoroughly, remove the shell, cut the egg into sections, and serve with soy sauce.
To Store: Thousand-year eggs can be kept up to a month in the refrigerator.

TIGER LILY BUDS (also known as Golden Needles) are dried lily buds, light gold in color and delicate in taste, used for flavor in some meat dishes and as a vegetable. Sold dried by the ounce, they are available in Chinese food stores or by mail. They must be soaked before adding to a recipe.
To Soak: Wash in cold water, then soak for 30 minutes in warm water, rinse, and cut off the tough stems.
To Store: Store dry in a covered container on the pantry shelf.
Substitution: None.

TREE EAR. See *Mushrooms, Tree Ear*.

VINEGAR. See *Rice Vinegar*.

WATER CHESTNUTS are not from a tree but are bulb-shaped stalks of an Asian water plant. They have a tough outer brown skin and an ivory white interior. The meat has a delicate flavor and a crisp crunchy texture when cooked quickly in a stir-fried recipe. Fresh water chestnuts are available at

Chinese food stores and in some specialty food departments. Canned water chestnuts are available in many supermarkets or by mail. As with many vegetables, canned water chestnuts don't compare with fresh ones for flavor but they will do as an alternative. To use fresh water chestnuts, wash thoroughly, peel off the brown skin, and slice the white meat thinly.

To Store: Fresh water chestnuts can be stored unpeeled in a plastic bag in the refrigerator for up to two weeks. When you have opened canned water chestnuts, store the remaining ones in water in a closed container in the refrigerator. Change the water every other day and they will keep for two or three weeks.

Substitution: Celery will add somewhat the same texture to a dish but canned water chestnuts are so widely available that you shouldn't need to make this substitution.

WINE. See *Rice Wine*.

WINTER MELON is a pale green-skinned vegetable the size of a pumpkin. The interior is white in color, crisp in texture, and delicate in flavor, but not sweet as would be expected of a "melon." Actually, it is a kind of squash. Winter melon can be used as a vegetable in stir-fried dishes or in the special Winter Melon Soup. Winter melon can be bought fresh (whole or in slices) in Chinese food stores. To use it in cooking, cut off the tough outer skin, scrape out the seeds, and cut up as directed in the recipe.

To Store: Cover winter melon slices with plastic wrap and refrigerate. They will keep a few days in the refrigerator.

Substitution: Cucumber.

WON TON SKINS OR WRAPPERS. See *Egg Roll Skins or Wrappers*.

TEA

In China tea is not just an incidental accompaniment to a meal. In fact, at most family meals in China it is not drunk during a meal at all.

Tea is served at various times during the day: at a tea break at home or at work; in a teahouse; as a special drink to welcome guests; or after a meal. Good tea is prized in China in the way that a fine wine or a special cognac is in France. The quality and flavor of tea, like wine, varies with its growing conditions. Tea connoisseurs will pay up to hundreds of dollars per pound for the rarest and best of teas.

There are literally hundreds of different varieties of Chinese tea, but they can be categorized into three basic types: green, black, and oolong.

Green tea is made from the tenderest leaves of the plant, which are dried immediately after they are picked. The leaves are not fermented. Green tea has a fresh, light taste.

Black tea (called red tea in China because, even though the leaves are black, the color of the brewed tea is red) is made from leaves that have been allowed to ferment. This produces a stronger-flavored, more aromatic tea.

Oolong tea is made from partially fermented tea leaves. The leaves are brownish green in color. The flavor of oolong tea is in between that of green and black tea.

The Chinese will frequently mix flower or fruit blossoms with tea to produce scented teas. Of these, jasmine tea is the best known. There are also smoked teas, such as lapsang souchong, but these are less popular in China.

The choice of which tea to serve depends on the individual and the occasion. The more aromatic teas, like burgundy wine, would generally be better with heavier foods, after dinner, or whenever a brisk taste is in order. The lighter green teas would be best at those times when a more delicate flavor is wanted.

There are some very definite guidelines to follow if you want to enjoy tea the Chinese way.

Buy the best-quality tea that your budget will allow. Store the tea in a closed glass, metal, or plastic container. Make sure your teapot is clean, but clean it only with water, not with soap. Use only water that is fresh from the tap, not water that has been standing in a teakettle or pan. Or, if you have it available use bottled spring water. Follow the brewing method that is described in Menu Lesson 1 of this book. Bring the water you will use to brew the tea just to a good, full boil—try not to under-boil it or overboil it; that really makes a difference in the taste and color of the tea you brew. Serve the tea hot. Definitely count on brewing two pots of tea from the same set of tea leaves (some connoisseurs consider the second brewing to have a better flavor). Remember that the Chinese drink their tea straight; they do not use cream, sugar, or lemon.

HOW TO GROW BEAN SPROUTS

You can easily grow bean sprouts yourself. Better yet, it is a good project for a child.

You can buy a simple bean sprouter in many health food stores or create one of your own. You only need something that will allow water to pass through, a colander or a perforated pan, and some cheesecloth.

The Chinese generally use soybeans, but most often the bean sprouts used here, even in Chinese restaurants, are from mung beans. The sprouts from mung beans are smaller than soybean sprouts.

You can buy mung beans at a health food store or Chinese food store, and a pound will last you quite a while.

Wash about 4 tablespoons of beans thoroughly and soak them overnight in warm water. They will swell to double their original size. In the morning rinse the beans several times until the rinse water remains clear. If you are using a colander or perforated pan, spread two layers of cheesecloth on the surface of it. Have the pan sitting in another pan or basin to catch over-flow water. Sprinkle the cloth with warm water so that it is moist and spread the mung beans evenly on the cloth. Cover the beans with another double layer of cheesecloth and moisten that evenly with warm water.

Place the beans in their sprouter in a dark place, in the base-ment or a closet, with a temperature of about 70°, give or take a few degrees. Darkness keeps the sprouts white in color. A tem-perature of approximately 70° best furthers the sprouting process.

Sprinkle the cheesecloth with warm water every 4 hours for the next 3 or 4 days to keep the beans moist (nighttime watering is not necessary). The excess water will drain away into the pan.

After the 3 or 4 days the sprouts should be 1½ to 2 inches long and ready for harvesting. If they are not yet that long, which may be the case if the room is too cool, leave them for another day.

Then immerse the sprouts in a pan of very cold water to separate any loose husks. Skim off and throw away the loose husks. The sprouts are then ready to be used. Sprouts not used the first day can be kept in water in the refrigerator for up to 4 or 5 days. You should change the water every day.

If you prefer to have soybean sprouts, follow the same process, using soy beans, but allow them to sprout for 6 or 7 days. The sprouts will be about 3 inches long at that time. The husks on soybean sprouts are tougher than those of mung bean sprouts, so you will have to wash them off by immersing them several times in cold water.

THE REGIONAL
COOKING OF CHINA

To most Westerners, Chinese cooking means Cantonese cooking. The majority of early emigrants from China to the United States were from the city of Canton and its neighboring provinces. The restaurants they opened naturally specialized in the cooking they knew best and to this day most of the Chinese restaurants outside of China are Cantonese.

In recent years, however, as interest in Chinese cooking has grown, the other regional cuisines of China—Szechuan and Peking particularly—have also gained much popularity.

It can be said that, gastronomically as well as geographically, China can be divided into four relatively separate regions:

NORTH

The cooking of the North, centered in the old imperial capital of Peking and the province of Shantung, is subtly seasoned and delicate. Wheat, more than rice, is the staple grain; it is used widely in dumplings, noodle dishes, buns, breads. On the scale of rare to well-done, the cooking of meats in the North tends to be in the medium range.

Peking, the center of the government for many centuries, attracted great chefs from all over China to serve the emperors and the mandarins, the officials of government. The diversity and elegance of the great banquets prepared for the emperors helped to shape the great cuisine of Peking. In American restaurants the term "Mandarin" is sometimes used interchangeably with "Peking," or more broadly, used to suggest the very best and most elegant of the cooking of China, fit for the mandarins. Examples of the best-known dishes of the North are Peking Duck, Scallion Pancakes, and Mu Shu Pork.

WEST

In contrast with the subtly seasoned cooking of the North, the cooking of the West is hot and spicy. Foods from the mountainous western province of Szechuan and the more central province of Hunan contain many of the same peppers found in Mexican and Indian food, and scallions, garlic, and ginger combine to create a very special kind of Chinese cooking, peppery hot in flavor yet still delicate in its taste. Szechuan recipes tend to use more meat, usually chicken or pork, and call for longer cooking than those of Peking or Canton. Examples of well-known Szechuan dishes are Kung Pao Chicken with Peanuts, Double-Cooked Pork, and Ants Climbing a Tree. Some special Hunan dishes are steamed or fried freshwater fish with a spicy sauce and hot peppery pork or chicken dishes.

SOUTH

The cooking of the South, centered in the port city of Canton, is, as has been said, the best known of the regional cuisines of China. The Cantonese style is to cook food only the minimum amount of time necessary—vegetables are still crisp, meats are tender and just done (but not rare). Quick-cooking methods like stir-frying, blanching, deep frying, and steaming are popular. Sauces are somewhat thicker in consistency than in Peking or Szechuan. Cantonese cooking, with access to the whole range of meats, poultry, fish, seafood, vegetables, and condiments, probably has the greatest diversity of all the regional cuisines of China, and certainly a great reputation for quality both in China (there are Cantonese restaurants all over China) and outside. Some special Cantonese dishes are Barbecued Spareribs and Pork Strips, Egg Fu Yung, and Winter Melon Soup.

EAST

The cooking of the East is less well known outside China and includes the cities of Yangchow, Shanghai, Ningpo, and the province of Fukien. The food is generally richer and more salty than elsewhere. Soy sauce and sugar are widely used. The cooking of Shanghai is perhaps closer to a national cuisine because it bears much influence from great chefs who have come from the other regions of China, a reflection of Shanghai's long-time status as China's most cosmopolitan city. Examples of typical eastern dishes are Soy Chicken, Fragrant Sliced Beef, and Drunken Chicken.

In this book we will bring you recipes for dishes that represent all of the regions of China, but with a particular concentration on the foods of Peking and, secondarily, Szechuan because of the growing new interest in these. Of course, many dishes are found in one variation or another all over China, so not all of the recipes are specifically identified with one particular region.

The menus in this book will often combine dishes from different regions. This reflects a basic fact of Chinese cooking, and a good part of the joy of it—variety is the true spice of eating. A Chinese meal can, and does, combine foods that are sweet and sour, bland and spicy, smooth and crunchy, hot and cold, from classic recipes and new creations. Just let your own good taste be your guide.

SIX MENU LESSONS

A BASIC COURSE
IN CHINESE COOKING

We begin the menu section of this book with a special selection of six menus that have been planned specifically as an instruction course in Chinese cooking. We give you detailed step-by-step instructions for both the preparation and cooking stages of each recipe. The menu lessons progress from a simple meal for two to a banquet for eight. You will have a chance to use most of the important ingredients in the Chinese cuisine. You will try recipes from the different regions of China and see how they differ.

We hope and believe you will finish these six lessons with the confidence and competence needed to make Chinese cooking a special part of your life. If you already know the techniques of Chinese cooking, you can skim over the instructional part of these lessons. In either case, the menus stand on their own as six meals carefully planned, as we have said earlier, to be manageable in the kitchen and great on the table.

Before we start the menu lessons, here are some general recipe notes.

QUANTITIES Stir-fried recipes in this book are designed to serve two or three people with full portions, or six to eight people with smaller portions, if the dish is to be included with a number of other dishes. In non-stir-fry recipes the number of people who can be served is indicated in the recipe.

ABOUT DESSERTS The Chinese generally do not have desserts, so there are relatively few that are a normal part of Chinese cooking. We have included a sweet ending for each of the first six menus but that pretty much covers our Chinese dessert repertoire. The rest of the menus and recipes following the lessons do not include desserts. If you wish to have a dessert with one of the later menus just use one from the menu lessons.

EQUIPMENT NEEDED As an added aid the specific pots and pans to be used for each recipe are listed at the beginning of each menu lesson.

ORGANIZATION Here are some special approaches we have followed in the presentation of recipes to make them as easy as possible to prepare:

TITLE The name of the recipe and the region from which it comes is listed, as well as the amount of marinating time (if the food is to be marinated) and preparation and cooking times. (NOTE: Food can be marinated longer than the time given—up to 24 hours if it is covered and refrigerated.) These times will help you in selecting a recipe and in allotting enough time to prepare it. Of course, these times are just approximate, because not everyone works at the same pace and not everyone's cooking equipment heats at the same rate.

DESCRIPTION Next we will give any special information you should know about the dish, e.g., what it looks like or tastes like and special tips that will help you in preparing or serving the dish.

INGREDIENTS Each ingredient listed in the recipe is described in detail in the ingredients section, and you should refer to that section before you begin to prepare the dish. To help you further, we have arranged certain ingredients into specifically identified groups in a recipe, for example, a marinade, vegetable combination, seasoning mixture, or special sauce. We have indicated which ingredients are to be minced, chopped, shredded, etc., so that when the time comes to cook, only the most brief and simple instructions are necessary.

"ON THE TRAY" This is an aid in stir-frying or in other recipes that call for cooking ingredients just a minute or two. We suggest you get ready by putting the proper quantities of individual ingredients or groups of ingredients (e.g., a sauce) in separate cups or bowls lined up on a tray in the order in which they will be used in the cooking process. This will assure that you have everything completely ready to follow the fast pace of the last-minute cooking in the wok without complication or overcooking. In the case of peanut oil, dry sherry, or sesame oil, we will suggest that you put the bottle on the tray rather than measuring out a small amount into a cup in advance.

TO PREPARE AND COOK The cooking procedure has been divided into two stages: "To Prepare" and "To Cook." "To Prepare" contains detailed step-by-step preparations for cooking. "To Cook" contains the specific cooking instructions in an easy-to-follow format.

For stir-fry dishes the recipe will tell you that the wok must be heated before adding the peanut oil. This will give you a hot, slick surface on which to cook. Next the oil must be heated before adding the food. This will prevent the food from absorbing the oil. In cooking beef or poultry, stir-fry just until the meat loses its pink color. Always cook pork a little longer to be sure that it is thoroughly done.

In recipes that require cornstarch we remind you to stir the dissolved cornstarch before adding it to the sauce. This is because the cornstarch will have settled in the water it has been combined with.

ADVANCE PREPARATION SCHEDULE To help you in planning the time you will need to prepare and cook your Chinese meals, we have also included as a separate section in the six menu lessons a proposed time schedule for that menu. The schedule will tell you how much of the preparation and cooking can be done in advance and which dishes can be refrigerated or frozen to be then reheated when they are served. The schedule will also serve as a checklist for organizing the final cooking of your meal.

MENU LESSON 1

AN INTRODUCTION TO STIR-FRYING

A SIMPLE BUT SUBLIME MENU FOR TWO

Egg Drop Soup
Mongolian Beef
Boiled Rice
Green Tea
Chinese Fruit

In this first dinner for two you will make a very simple but delicious soup, a stir-fried beef dish, and learn how to boil rice in the Chinese manner. You will want to experiment with a variety of teas. For this dinner we've chosen a green tea, light in color and subtle in flavor. There is a simple fruit dessert.

59

In preparing this and all the following menus we suggest that you first read through the entire menu and all the instructions that are a part of it. Refer back to the detailed ingredients listing that starts on page 23 when you need to know more information about the ingredients you will be using. Look at the schedule at the end of the lesson to help yourself organize the preparation and cooking of the meal.

NEW COOKING METHOD: STIR-FRYING

In this first meal you will learn the basic technique of stir-frying (chow), which simply means that the food is cooked quickly in a wok or a skillet over high heat in a small amount of oil.

In stir-frying it is important that the wok is hot before the oil is added, and then that the oil is hot before the food is added so that the food does not absorb the oil. The food should sizzle when placed in the oil. You will learn by experience when the oil is hot enough. You do not want the food to burn but you do want it to cook quickly. While cooking, the food is stirred constantly and tossed with a spatula so that it all cooks quickly and evenly. The entire surface of the pan is a cooking surface and the rounded bottom makes it easier to toss the food. If vegetables and meat are to be combined, they are stir-fried separately; usually the meat is cooked first, then it is removed from the wok and the vegetables are cooked. They are then combined with the sauce to complete the dish. The trick is to have all your ingredients lined up on a tray in the order in which they are to be added to the pan. Then you can work quickly and efficiently.

If you are using a gas stove it is easier to control the cooking time—you merely turn off the flame when the cooking is completed. On an electric stove, because the coils continue to be hot for some time after the burner is switched off, it is necessary to remove your pan from the burner when the cooking time is up to prevent the food from overcooking—an important thing to avoid in Chinese stir-frying. The objective is to keep the meat juicy and the vegetables crisp when stir-frying.

Stir-frying is the most widely used of the Chinese cooking

methods, probably because it is the most economical. The wood and coal used as cooking fuels in China were scarce and costly so a very quick method of cooking was developed. Stir-frying has the added advantage of retaining most of the nutrients in food because the cooking time is so short.

In this meal you will also begin your use of the Chinese cleaver in preparing the Mongolian Beef recipe. Please refer back to pages 12–13 and 16–17 for basic information on the cleaver and for instructions in the use of the cleaver.

COOKING EQUIPMENT NEEDED

For the Egg Drop Soup: a 2-quart saucepan
For the Mongolian Beef: a wok or skillet
For the rice: a 2-quart saucepan

PREPARATION AND COOKING
OF THE MEAL

EGG DROP SOUP

PREPARATION TIME: 10 MINUTES   ALL REGIONS
COOKING TIME: 5 MINUTES

Egg Drop Soup is a simple soup made with chicken broth, flavorings, cornstarch, an egg, and thinly sliced green scallion for color. Remember, in Chinese cooking appearance and texture are almost as important as flavor. The whole scallion is chopped and used as a garnish to add a bright green color to the dish. White pepper is used so there will not be any unsightly black specks in the soup, again indicating how important the visual appeal of the dish is to the Chinese cook.

3   *cups canned chicken broth*
¼   *teaspoon salt*
¼   *teaspoon white pepper*
½   *teaspoon sugar*

2   *teaspoons cornstarch, dissolved in 2 teaspoons
     cold water*

1   *teaspoon dry sherry*

1   *egg, lightly beaten*

1   *whole scallion, thinly sliced*

ON THE TRAY:
Saucepan containing broth, salt, pepper, sugar
Cup containing dissolved cornstarch
Bottle of dry sherry (NOTE: It is easier to pour from the bottle during cooking than to keep track of 1 teaspoon or tablespoon of liquid.)
Cup containing egg
Cup containing sliced scallion

TO COOK:
1. Heat seasoned broth just to boiling.

2. Stir cornstarch, which will have settled, and add to the broth.

3. Stir until the soup is thickened, about 1 minute.

4. Add sherry and stir.

5. With a chopstick or a wooden spoon gently stir the soup as you slowly pour in the egg. The egg will form delicate shreds in the soup.

6. Remove from the heat and garnish with scallions.

7. Serve immediately in individual bowls.

MONGOLIAN BEEF

MARINATING TIME: 20 MINUTES PEKING
PREPARATION TIME: 20 MINUTES
COOKING TIME: 5 MINUTES

This is one of the most popular dishes in Peter Wong's Mandarin Inn restaurant in Chinatown in New York City. It combines tender slices of beef and scallions with a ginger sauce.

When you purchase the flank steak for this recipe, trim off most of the fat and cut the meat lengthwise into 3 long strips, following the grain, about 1½ to 2 inches wide. Cut these strips with the cleaver (see page 17) at a 45° angle against the grain into ¼-inch-thick slices. To make the meat easier to slice you can put it into your freezer for 45 minutes and do the slicing when the meat is semifrozen. The secret of the tenderness of the beef is a combination of cross-grain slicing and marinating.

Peter Wong stirs a tiny bit of sesame oil into many of his dishes after they are cooked. We generally list it as optional. However, use it if you have it. You will find the oil adds a pleasant, nutlike flavor to the dish.

1 *pound flank steak, thinly sliced as described above into pieces ¼ × 1½ × 2 inches long*

MARINADE:
1   egg
¼   teaspoon salt
¼   teaspoon black pepper
1   teaspoon sugar
2   tablespoons cornstarch
1   tablespoon peanut oil

   ¼   cup peanut oil

   2   tablespoons peanut oil

SEASONINGS:
1   whole scallion, minced
1   teaspoon minced fresh ginger
1   teaspoon minced garlic

SAUCE:
2   tablespoons soy sauce
3   tablespoons dry sherry
1   tablespoon hoisin sauce
3   tablespoons water

   8   whole scallions cut into 2-inch pieces

   1   teaspoon sesame oil (optional)

TO PREPARE:
1. Mix the ingredients for the marinade in a bowl until smooth.

2. Put in the beef slices and set aside uncovered for at least 20 minutes. (They can be marinated up to 24 hours, covered, in the refrigerator.)

ON THE TRAY:
   Bottle of peanut oil
   Bowl containing marinated beef slices
   Cup containing seasonings: scallion, ginger, garlic
   Cup containing sauce mixed together: soy sauce, sherry, hoisin, and water
   Cup containing cut-up scallions
   Bottle of sesame oil

TO COOK:

1. Heat wok over high heat.
2. Add ¼ cup peanut oil.
3. When oil is hot, add meat and its marinade.
4. Stir-fry about 2 minutes or until the meat loses its pink color.
5. Remove meat from the wok and set aside in a bowl, uncovered.
6. Add 2 tablespoons peanut oil to the wok.
7. When the oil is hot, add the seasonings—minced scallion, ginger, and garlic.
8. Stir a few times, then add the sauce—soy sauce, sherry, hoisin sauce, and water mixed together.
9. Stir and add the scallion pieces.
10. Stir for ½ minute then return the beef to the wok.
11. Stir just to heat through.
12. Stir in sesame oil, if desired.
13. Remove wok from heat and serve immediately.

BOILED RICE

PREPARATION TIME: 2 MINUTES
COOKING TIME: 40 MINUTES

If you've had trouble cooking rice in the past, weep no more. This recipe for boiled rice is foolproof. The Chinese like their rice freshly cooked and unsalted. It is the basic staple of their diet, except in the northern regions such as Peking or Shantung where noodles might be served instead. In the following menus we will occasionally serve fried rice in place of plain boiled rice. This is a concession to Western practice. In China they generally serve plain rice in addition to the fried rice. Please know also that the Chinese do not use precooked rice, and neither should you.

This recipe makes 3 cups of rice. To double the quantity of cooked rice, use 2 cups of raw rice but only 3 cups of cold water.

1   cup long-grain rice
1¾ cups cold water

TO COOK:

1. Place rice in a saucepan and add cold water.
2. *Cover tightly.*
3. Bring to boil over highest heat.
4. When you see steam escaping, turn the heat very low but *do not remove cover.*
5. Set a timer for 20 minutes, cooking at this low heat.
6. Remove pan from heat but do not touch the cover.
7. Let the rice stand for another 20 minutes.
8. Fluff up with a fork or a chopstick before serving.
9. Plan the timing of the rice to coordinate with the rest of the dinner.
10. Serve rice in individual bowls. The bowls are refilled throughout the dinner.

GREEN TEA

PREPARATION TIME: 2 MINUTES
BREWING TIME: 3 MINUTES

Green tea is a very delicate tea made from unfermented leaves. To learn more about the various Chinese teas refer to the section on tea.

A second pot of tea can be brewed from the same tea leaves by adding more boiling water. Remember the Chinese drink their tea without cream, sugar, or lemon.

FOR TWO PEOPLE
2   *teaspoons tea*
4   *cups rapidly boiling water*

TO BREW:

1. Bring water to a rapid boil.
2. Measure 2 teaspoons of tea into a ceramic teapot.
3. Add 1 inch of boiling water.

4. Allow to steep for 3 minutes.
5. Add remainder of boiling water.
6. Serve.

NOTE: This brewing method is used for all Chinese teas in this book.

CHINESE FRUIT

CHILLING TIME: 1 HOUR

Dessert will be canned longans, lichees, or loquats. If these are unavailable, use fresh or canned pineapple chunks, mandarin oranges, or melon balls.

1. Chill fruit at least 1 hour before serving.
2. Serve fruit with its juice in individual bowls.

ADVANCE PREPARATION SUGGESTIONS
AND SCHEDULE

This schedule has two purposes: to give you a checklist and time-table for the cooking of this meal and to show you how much of the preparation for the meal can be done in advance if you wish to do so. Of course, the advance preparation suggestions are strictly optional. You may prefer to prepare and cook the whole meal on a normal predinner schedule; if so, just use the preparation and cooking times listed in each individual recipe to plan the time you will need.

A PREVIOUS DAY:

Cut the flank steak for the Mongolian Beef into 3 lengthwise strips following the grain, wrap it tightly in foil, and freeze it.

EARLY ON THE DAY OF THE DINNER:

1. Slightly thaw the flank steak. Now you can cut the steak into very thin slices and combine it with the marinade. (The meat can be cut fresh; freezing simply makes it easier to do.) Refrigerate.

2. Prepare the scallions, ginger, and garlic for the Mongolian Beef and the scallions for the Egg Drop Soup. Cover well and refrigerate.

3. Prepare the sauce for the Mongolian Beef in a bowl, cover, and refrigerate.

4. Place fruit in the refrigerator to chill.

40 MINUTES BEFORE DINNER:

Start the rice. Remember, it cooks for 20 minutes and then rests for another 20 minutes to absorb any excess liquid.

10 MINUTES BEFORE DINNER:

Heat chicken broth combined with salt, sugar, and pepper for the Egg Drop Soup.

5 MINUTES BEFORE DINNER:

1. Stir-fry the Mongolian Beef.
2. Start the water boiling for the Green Tea.

IMMEDIATELY BEFORE SERVING:

Stir into the boiling chicken broth the cornstarch, dry sherry, and beaten egg.

We hope you and your dinner partner have enjoyed your first Chinese cooking effort. You now have some beginning evidence of the great new food experience that Chinese cooking can be for you. As you think back on it, you will realize that you have learned a lot in just this first meal. And you are ready to carry on now to Menu Lesson 2. We suggest, if you want to make an event of it, that you set a specific night each week to be your Chinese dinner night. Then go through the menus in the following chapters on that special night. We think you'll look forward to it as a special treat each week.

MENU LESSON 2

CHINESE-STYLE OVEN-ROASTING
(And More Stir-Frying)

ANOTHER GREAT DINNER FOR TWO

Barbecued Spareribs
Hot Mustard Sauce and Duck Sauce
Chicken with Hoisin Sauce and Cashews
Boiled Rice
Black Tea
Orange-Pineapple Soup

In this second dinner for two you will prepare Barbecued Spare-ribs, always a favorite with Americans. If you prefer, they can be made ahead of time and reheated in the oven. In addition to the spareribs, we will have Chicken with Hoisin Sauce and

Cashews. This dish will give you additional practice in stir-frying and using the cleaver. We will again serve the boiled rice described in the preceding menu lesson. Black Tea is full-bodied and aromatic and goes well with our dinner. For dessert there is a special Chinese fruit soup that can be made ahead and reheated.

NEW COOKING METHOD: OVEN-ROASTING

In the Chinese method of oven-roasting the meat cooks above a pan that contains water. The steam from the water keeps the meat juicy and the water in the pan catches the drippings from the meat and prevents the oven from smoking. Often the Chinese will roast meat suspended on hooks from the top of the oven over a pan, but we will use a pan fitted with a rack. Fill the pan with 2 cups of water and place the meat that is to be roasted on the rack. (Be sure that the meat does not touch the water.) During the cooking turn the meat so that it becomes evenly browned. Most recipes will call for basting the meat with a sauce or marinade.

COOKING EQUIPMENT NEEDED

For the Barbecued Spareribs: a deep oven-roasting pan fitted with rack

For the Chicken with Hoisin Sauce and Cashews: a wok or skillet

For the rice: a 2-quart saucepan

For the Orange-Pineapple Soup: a 2-quart saucepan

PREPARATION AND COOKING
OF THE MEAL

BARBECUED SPARERIBS

PREPARATION TIME: 10 MINUTES   CANTON
MARINATING TIME: 2–3 HOURS
COOKING TIME: 1 HOUR AND 20 MINUTES

The Chinese style of oven-roasting minimizes the greasiness that is often associated with American baked spareribs. When you purchase the ribs, ask your butcher for small, tender ones that have been trimmed of most of the fat and gristle. You will know why Barbecued Spareribs, Cantonese style, are such a popular dish for many people after you have marinated and basted them in the savory sauce, and cooked them this classic way.

1   slab (about 2 pounds) of fresh young spareribs

MARINADE:
4   tablespoons soy sauce
4   tablespoons hoisin sauce
2   tablespoons dry sherry
¼   teaspoon 5-spice powder
2   tablespoons honey

TO PREPARE:

1. Mix all the ingredients of the marinade together in a bowl.

2. Brush the meat on both sides with the marinade mixture.

3. Put the ribs (whole) into a large pan and pour over the remaining marinade.

4. Set aside 2 or 3 hours at room temperature or overnight, covered, in the refrigerator.

TO COOK:

1. Set oven at 375°.

2. Pour 2 cups of water into the bottom of the roasting pan.

3. Drain meat, saving the remainder of the marinade, and place on rack.

4. Place rack with meat on it in the pan in the oven. *Do not let ribs touch the water.*

5. After 30 minutes brush both sides of ribs with marinade and turn over.

6. After 1 hour total cooking time remove ribs from oven and pour off water.

7. Raise oven heat to 450°.

8. Put roasting pan and rack with meat back in the oven and brown on both sides, turning after about 8–10 minutes.

9. Remove from oven in approximately 20 minutes.

TO SERVE:

1. Cut into individual ribs to be eaten with the fingers.

2. Heap ribs on a large platter and serve with Hot Mustard and Duck Sauces.

HOT MUSTARD SAUCE

PREPARATION TIME: 5 MINUTES   CANTON
CHILLING TIME: 24 HOURS

Both of the following sauces go well with a variety of Chinese foods. You will notice we suggest using them with several of the recipes in this book.

The mustard gets stronger as it sits. So, if you can, make it at least 1 day ahead for more flavor. Both the Hot Mustard and the Duck Sauces will keep for weeks in a covered jar in the refrigerator.

¼ *cup dry mustard powder*
¼ *cup cold water*
1   *teaspoon white rice vinegar*
¼ *teaspoon salt*

TO PREPARE:

1. Mix mustard powder with 2 tablespoons of cold water and blend into a smooth paste.

2. Add the remaining cold water gradually.

3. Add the rice vinegar and the salt. (It should be a smooth, thin sauce.)

4. Cover tightly and refrigerate.

DUCK SAUCE

PREPARATION TIME: 10 MINUTES   CANTON

  1   cup mango chutney
  1   cup apricot preserves
  ¼   cup cold water

TO PREPARE:

1. Chop chutney coarsely with your cleaver.

2. Mix chutney with the preserves and the water.

3. Cover tightly and refrigerate.

CHICKEN WITH HOISIN SAUCE AND CASHEWS

MARINATING TIME: 20 MINUTES   SHANTUNG
PREPARATION TIME: 20 MINUTES
COOKING TIME: 5 MINUTES

This dish combines tender pieces of boneless chicken with vegetables and cashews in a sweet bean sauce. Preparation of this dish will require the use of a cleaver (or heavy kitchen knife) for chopping. When preparing the various ingredients cut them into uniform pieces. In this recipe the pieces are diced or cut into ½-inch cubes. The reasons for uniformity in shape and size are to enable all the ingredients to cook evenly, to simplify eating the food with chopsticks, and to produce a more pleasing appearance.

Do not cook this dish ahead because the vegetables will lose their crispness. However, if you have all the ingredients ready and set up on a tray as suggested, it will be a simple task to stir-fry at the last minute.

  2   whole chicken breasts, boned, skinned, and diced into
       ½-inch cubes

MARINADE:

1   egg
1   tablespoon soy sauce
1   tablespoon dry sherry
1   tablespoon cornstarch
½   teaspoon salt

   3   tablespoons peanut oil

   1   tablespoon peanut oil

VEGETABLES:

½   cup diced canned water chestnuts
½   cup diced green pepper
½   cup diced fresh or canned mushrooms

   2   tablespoons hoisin sauce

   ½   cup roasted cashews, unsalted

TO PREPARE:

   1. Mix the ingredients for the marinade in a bowl until smooth.

   2. Put in the diced chicken and mix well with marinade. Set aside uncovered for at least 20 minutes. (The chicken can be marinated up to 24 hours, covered, in the refrigerator.)

ON THE TRAY:

   Bottle of peanut oil
   Bowl containing marinated chicken
   Bowl containing diced vegetables
   Hoisin sauce
   Cup containing cashews

TO COOK:

   1. Heat wok or skillet over high heat.
   2. Add 3 tablespoons peanut oil.
   3. When oil is hot, add marinated chicken.
   4. Stir-fry for 2 minutes or until chicken loses its pink color.
   5. Remove chicken from wok and set aside in a bowl.
   6. In the same wok heat 1 tablespoon peanut oil.
   7. Add vegetables and stir-fry 1 minute.
   8. Return chicken to wok and stir.
   9. Add hoisin sauce and mix well.

10. Add cashew nuts.
11. Stir-fry 1 minute until food is heated through.
12. Remove wok from heat and serve immediately.

BOILED RICE

PREPARATION TIME: 2 MINUTES
COOKING TIME: 40 MINUTES

See Menu Lesson 1.

BLACK TEA

PREPARATION TIME: 2 MINUTES
BREWING TIME: 3 MINUTES

See recipe for Green Tea in Menu Lesson 1.

ORANGE-PINEAPPLE SOUP

PREPARATION TIME: 10 MINUTES
COOKING TIME: 5 MINUTES

A sweet, hot soup is sometimes served for dessert in China. We include a recipe so that you may try it.

½ cup canned mandarin oranges, drained
½ cup canned pineapple tidbits, drained
2   cups water
¼ cup sugar
1   tablespoon cornstarch, dissolved in 2 tablespoons
    cold water

TO COOK:
1. Bring water to a boil.
2. Add sugar and stir until it is dissolved.
3. Stir cornstarch and add.
4. Stir until thickened, about 1 minute.
5. Add fruit.
6. Stir about 1 minute until soup is heated through.
7. Serve warm in individual bowls.

ADVANCE PREPARATION SUGGESTIONS
AND SCHEDULE

A PREVIOUS DAY:

1. Marinate the spareribs 2–3 hours at room temperature or overnight in the refrigerator.

2. Roast the spareribs. Wrap tightly in foil and refrigerate them up to 2 or 3 days, or you can freeze them.

3. Make Duck Sauce and Hot Mustard Sauce. Cover and refrigerate.

EARLIER ON THE DAY OF THE DINNER:

1. Dice the boned chicken and combine with the marinade. Cover and refrigerate.

2. Dice all the vegetables to be added to the Chicken with Hoisin Sauce and Cashews. Cover and refrigerate.

3. Make the Orange-Pineapple Soup, but do not add cornstarch. Cover and refrigerate.

40 MINUTES BEFORE DINNER:

Start the rice.

20 MINUTES BEFORE DINNER:

Heat the foil-wrapped ribs at 350°. (If frozen, heat for 45 minutes.) It is not necessary to unwrap them.

5 MINUTES BEFORE DINNER:

1. Stir-fry the Chicken with Hoisin Sauce and Cashews.

2. Start water boiling for the tea.

3. Reheat the Orange-Pineapple Soup and add cornstarch.

MENU LESSON 3

THE CHINESE METHOD OF DEEP FRYING (And Again Stir-Frying)

A DIVERSIFIED DINNER FOR FOUR

Egg Rolls
Corn Soup
Mandarin Sweet and Pungent Pork
Watercress Salad with Water Chestnuts
Boiled Rice
Oolong Tea
Almond Float

Now you are ready to tackle a dinner for four people. Although we have added extra dishes to accommodate four, you will see that much of the preparation can be done ahead. The technique

78

of deep frying will be used for cooking both the Egg Rolls and the pork in the sweet and sour dish. We have included a cold dish, a soup, and a dessert that can all be made well in advance. We will sample Oolong Tea and serve Almond Float (or Almond Junket, as it is sometimes called) for dessert.

NEW COOKING METHOD: DEEP FRYING

In this method the food is cooked in hot oil. The oil must be deep enough so that the food floats in it. The Chinese traditionally use lard or peanut oil for all their frying. We will use peanut oil in this book. It is expensive but has many advantages. It does not smoke when heated to very high temperatures. It does not take on the flavors of the foods cooked in it so it can be used several times, and it does not turn rancid if it is not refrigerated.

Because food is deep fried at a specific temperature, it is important to use either a deep-fat frying thermometer or an electric frying pan or deep-fat fryer so that you maintain the correct temperature while frying. To maintain the correct temperature once it is reached, do not cook too many pieces of food at one time because as the food is added the temperature of the oil drops slightly. If the oil is not hot enough, the food absorbs too much oil and becomes greasy. Do not add any food until the oil reaches its correct temperature again. Drain the fried foods on paper towels before serving.

Because each cook's fryer will heat at different time rates, the approximate cooking times may vary. Also, if you fry fewer pieces at one time it will take you longer to cook the food.

Restaurants often use a method called double-frying or frying twice. You may do this at home if you wish. It makes the food much crisper. The food is fried, drained, and refrigerated until mealtime, then it is quickly fried again for just a minute or two to crisp it.

COOKING EQUIPMENT NEEDED

For the Egg Rolls: an electric deep-fat fryer or an electric frying pan, or a deep 4-quart saucepan and a cooking thermometer

For the Corn Soup: a 2-quart saucepan

For the Mandarin Sweet and Pungent Pork: an electric deep-fat fryer or electric frying pan, or a deep 4-quart saucepan and a cooking thermometer. And a wok or 2-quart saucepan in which to parboil the broccoli and carrots and to prepare the sweet and sour sauce.

For the Watercress Salad with Water Chestnuts: a 4-quart saucepan for blanching and a large mixing bowl

For the rice: a 2-quart saucepan

For the Almond Float: a square 8 × 8-inch pan

PREPARATION AND COOKING
OF THE MEAL

EGG ROLLS

PREPARATION TIME: 1 HOUR AND 45 MINUTES   CANTON
COOKING TIME: 10 MINUTES

Egg Rolls are made of chopped meat and/or seafood and vegetables wrapped in a casing made of dough and then deep fried.
The casing around the egg roll is called the wrapper or the skin.
Ready-made egg roll skins are often available in special food
stores and they are usually good. By all means buy them if they
are available. If not, use the recipe given below.

Use fresh shrimp, or, if you wish to save yourself a lot of
work, buy an 8-ounce bag of frozen, uncooked, shelled and deveined shrimp. Disregard the cooking directions on the bag; they
generally advise you to overcook the shrimp. Bring 2 quarts of
water to a boil, add shrimp, bring to a boil again and immediately
drain. Rinse with cold water to prevent further cooking.

Serve egg rolls to your guests while they are having cocktails or as a first course. Cut each egg roll into 3 pieces for
easier handling and serve with the Hot Mustard and Duck Sauces
given in Menu Lesson 2.

EGG ROLL SKINS (*makes about 1 dozen*)

2   *cups all-purpose flour*
½   *teaspoon salt*
1   *egg, lightly beaten*
½–¾ *cup water*

TO PREPARE:

1. Combine flour and salt in a large bowl.

2. Add egg and gradually add water.

3. Knead with your hands about 10 minutes until the dough
is soft and elastic.

4. Cover with a damp dish towel and set aside 15 minutes.

5. Roll half the dough out onto a generously floured board
as thin as you can.

6. Cut into 6-inch squares and continue rolling until it measures 8 × 8 inch. Flour each skin so they will not stick together, and stack until you are ready to use them. (Skins can be wrapped in foil and refrigerated up to 3 days or frozen until ready to use.)

7. Repeat using remaining dough.

EGG ROLLS

2   *tablespoons peanut oil*

FILLING:
½ *pound lean, ground pork*
½ *pound shrimp, cooked, shelled, deveined, and coarsely*
    chopped
½ *pound bean sprouts, chopped*
8   *whole scallions, chopped*
1   *tablespoon soy sauce*
½ *teaspoon salt*

1   *egg, lightly beaten*

4   *cups peanut oil for deep frying*

1   *dozen egg roll skins (see preceding recipe)*

TO COOK:
1. Heat wok or skillet over high heat.
2. Add 2 tablespoons peanut oil.
3. When oil is hot add pork.
4. Turn to medium heat and stir-fry 3 minutes or until the pork loses its pink color.
5. Add shrimp, bean sprouts, scallions and stir-fry 1 minute.
6. Add soy sauce and salt and stir.
7. Remove wok from heat and allow filling to cool before assembling the egg rolls.

TO ASSEMBLE THE EGG ROLLS:
1. Cover the egg roll skins with a slightly dampened cloth to prevent them from drying out while you are working.
2. Carefully peel off 1 egg roll skin.
3. Place on a lightly floured board with one corner pointing toward you.

4. Using a slotted spoon (so the filling won't be too wet and split the egg roll skin) place about 2 tablespoons of the filling below the center of the skin.

5. With a pastry brush, paint the outer edge of the skin with the beaten egg.

6. Fold over the front edge of the skin to cover the filling, then fold in the end flaps.

7. Now roll from the bottom until you have a cylinder. The beaten egg will glue the wrapper closed.

8. Place sealed side down on a plate.

9. Cover filled egg rolls with a damp dish towel until ready to fry.

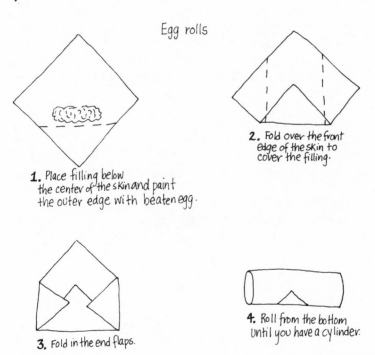

Egg rolls

1. Place filling below the center of the skin and paint the outer edge with beaten egg.

2. Fold over the front edge of the skin to cover the filling.

3. Fold in the end flaps.

4. Roll from the bottom until you have a cylinder.

TO FRY:

1. Heat 4 cups of peanut oil to 375° in a deep-fat fryer or an electric frying pan. (See page 79 for basic deep-frying instructions.)

2. Fry egg rolls, 4 at a time, about 3 minutes, until golden.

3. Drain on paper towels.

4. Reserve cooking oil in a covered jar to be used another time.

NOTE: This recipe makes approximately 12 egg rolls. In a dinner for four you may want to serve only 4 or 6 and freeze the others to be used another time.

CORN SOUP

PREPARATION TIME: 10 MINUTES   SHANTUNG
COOKING TIME: 5 MINUTES

This delicious soup has a smooth texture and a delicate flavor. It is not difficult to make but the timing is critical because the cornstarch and the egg whites must be added immediately before serving. It is the beaten egg whites that give the soup its smooth, velvety consistency.

4   *cups canned chicken broth*
1   *8-ounce can creamed corn*
¼   *teaspoon salt*
1½   *tablespoons cornstarch, dissolved in 3 tablespoons*
     cold water
1   *tablespoon dry sherry*
2   *egg whites, beaten until fluffy*
1   *whole scallion, thinly sliced*

TO COOK:

1. Bring chicken broth to a boil.

2. Add salt and creamed corn.

3. Stir constantly and bring to a boil again.

4. Stir dissolved cornstarch, which will have settled, then add to the soup.

5. Stir until the soup is thickened, about 1 minute.

6. Add sherry and stir.

7. Remove soup from the heat and add egg whites, stirring gently.

8. Garnish with scallion and serve immediately in individual bowls.

MANDARIN SWEET AND PUNGENT PORK

PREPARATION TIME: 45 MINUTES   CANTON
COOKING TIME: 20 MINUTES

The secret of a good sweet and sour dish is to deep fry the meat or seafood first in a light batter, then combine it with the sauce just before serving. This preserves the crispness of the meat or seafood. In this case, the pork cubes can be fried well ahead of time and then refried briefly to recrisp them just before serving. (See page 79.) The sauce, too, can be made ahead and reheated, but do not add the cornstarch thickener until just before serving or it will become gluey.

1   *pound lean pork, cut into 1-inch cubes*

BATTER:
1   *egg, lightly beaten*
1   *tablespoon dry sherry*
1   *tablespoon cornstarch*
2   *tablespoons flour*
½   *teaspoon salt*

4   *cups peanut oil for deep frying*

2   *tablespoons peanut oil*

VEGETABLES:
2   *medium carrots, sliced*
8   *small broccoli flowers*
8   *dried Chinese mushrooms, soaked in warm water 30 minutes*

SEASONINGS:
1   *teaspoon minced fresh ginger*
½   *teaspoon minced garlic*

SAUCE:
1   *cup canned chicken broth*
½   *teaspoon chili paste with garlic*
3   *tablespoons sugar*
1   *tablespoon soy sauce*
3   *tablespoons white rice vinegar*
3   *tablespoons tomato catsup*

1   *tablespoon cornstarch, dissolved in 2 tablespoons
    cold water*

TO PREPARE:

1. Combine ingredients for batter and mix well until smooth.

2. Add pork cubes, mix well, and place in the refrigerator 30 minutes before deep frying.

3. Bring 2 quarts of water to a boil and add carrots and broccoli. Boil 2 minutes, drain, and rinse in cold water.

4. Rinse mushrooms, discard tough stems, and cut into quarters.

ON THE TRAY:

Bottle of peanut oil
Bowl containing pork in batter
Cup containing seasonings—ginger and garlic
Bowl containing vegetables
Bowl containing sauce mixed together
Cup containing dissolved cornstarch

TO COOK:

Step 1:

1. Heat 4 cups peanut oil to 350° in a deep-fat fryer. (See page 79 for basic deep-frying instructions.)

2. Add pork half at a time and fry about 6 minutes until golden brown.

3. Drain on paper towels.

4. You may keep the pork warm in a low, 200° oven until the sauce is ready.

5. Reserve the oil in a covered jar to be used another time.

Step 2:

1. Heat wok or skillet over high heat.

2. Add 2 tablespoons peanut oil.

3. When oil is hot, add seasonings and stir.

4. Add vegetables and stir.

5. Add sauce and stir until boiling.

6. Stir dissolved cornstarch, which will have settled, and add to mixture.

7. Stir until thickened, about 1 minute.
8. Add cooked pork to the sauce.
9. Remove from heat and serve immediately.

WATERCRESS SALAD WITH WATER CHESTNUTS

PREPARATION TIME: 15 MINUTES   PEKING
CHILLING TIME: 1 HOUR

A plus for this dish is that it is served cold and can be made early in the day and chilled. The watercress has a peppery bite to it that adds a bit of tang to your dinner.

2   *bunches of watercress*
12 *canned water chestnuts, finely chopped*
1   *teaspoon salt*
1   *tablespoon white rice vinegar*
2   *teaspoons sugar*
1   *tablespoon sesame oil*

TO PREPARE:
Step 1:
    1. Trim tougher stems from watercress and rinse in cold water.
    2. Bring 2 quarts of water to a boil.
    3. Add watercress and blanch for 1 minute.
    4. Drain and rinse in cold water.

Step 2:
    1. Squeeze watercress to get out excess water.
    2. Chop fine.
    3. Place in a mixing bowl and add remaining ingredients.
    4. Mix well.
    5. Chill at least 1 hour before serving.

BOILED RICE

PREPARATION TIME: 2 MINUTES
COOKING TIME: 40 MINUTES

See Menu Lesson 1.

OOLONG TEA

PREPARATION TIME: 2 MINUTES
BREWING TIME: 3 MINUTES

See recipe for Green Tea in Menu Lesson 1.

ALMOND FLOAT

PREPARATION TIME: 5 MINUTES   SHANGHAI
CHILLING TIME: 4 HOURS OR OVERNIGHT

This is a refreshing dessert often served at banquets. It is especially pleasing in the summertime. For a change you may add
strawberries, mandarin oranges, or fruit cocktail to the syrup.

2   *cups milk*
¼   *cup sugar*
1   *envelope unflavored gelatin, dissolved in ¼ cup*
    cold water
1   *tablespoon almond extract*

TO COOK:
1. Heat milk to just below boiling.
2. Add sugar and stir until it is dissolved.
3. Add gelatin and stir until it is completely mixed in.
4. Stir in almond extract.
5. Pour into an 8 × 8-inch pan and cover.
6. Chill about 4 hours in the refrigerator until solid.
7. Serve with the syrup given below.

SYRUP:

½ *cup sugar*
2 *cups warm water*
1 *teaspoon almond extract*

TO PREPARE:
1. Dissolve sugar in water.
2. Cool slightly in the refrigerator.
3. Add almond extract.
4. Cover and refrigerate at least 1 hour to chill.

TO SERVE:
1. Cut gelatin mixture into small squares and float in syrup.
2. Serve in individual rice bowls.

ADVANCE PREPARATION SUGGESTIONS
AND SCHEDULE

THE DAY BEFORE:

1. Prepare filling for the Egg Rolls, cover and refrigerate.
2. Prepare Egg Roll Skins, cover and refrigerate.
3. Prepare Almond Float and syrup, cover and refrigerate.

EARLY ON THE DAY OF THE DINNER:

1. Mix pork with batter. Set aside for 30 minutes.
2. Fry pork cubes, drain. Cover and refrigerate.
3. Chop vegetables for the Mandarin Sweet and Pungent Pork.
4. Prepare the sauce for the pork. (Do not add the cornstarch until just before serving.)
5. Assemble Egg Rolls. Fry, drain, cover and refrigerate.
6. Prepare Watercress Salad with Water Chestnuts. Cover and refrigerate.

40 MINUTES BEFORE DINNER:

1. Start the rice.
2. Refry Egg Rolls at 375° for 1 minute until crisp. Drain on paper towels. Serve with cocktails.

15 MINUTES BEFORE DINNER:

1. Refry pork cubes 1 minute at 375° until crisp. Keep warm in a low, 200° oven.
2. Reheat Sweet and Pungent Sauce. Add cornstarch to thicken.

10 MINUTES BEFORE DINNER:

Make the Corn Soup.

5 MINUTES BEFORE DINNER:

Start the water boiling for the tea.

MENU LESSON 4

STEAMING THE CHINESE WAY
(Deep Frying and Stir-Frying, Too)

A FEAST FOR FOUR

Shrimp-Stuffed Mushrooms in Oyster Sauce
Won Ton Soup
Fish Filet Hunan Style
Yang Chow Fried Rice
Cucumber Salad
Lichee Black Tea
Almond Cookies

In this second dinner for four people you will learn the Chinese method of steaming food when you prepare the stuffed mushrooms. You will make your own Won Tons for the soup. Fish Filet Hunan Style is pieces of white fish topped with a delicious spicy sauce typical of the Hunan region of western China. The Fried Rice, the Cucumber Salad, and the Almond Cookies can be made well ahead. Lichee Black Tea completes our menu.

NEW COOKING METHOD: STEAMING

Steaming is a very common method of preparing food in Chinese cooking. Vegetables, meats, seafood, and sometimes whole fish are steamed, while various spices and vegetables are added to create a great diversity of tastes. Also many of the *dim sum,* or assorted dumplings, are steamed. It is a marvelous way of cooking because all the vitamins and minerals are preserved rather than being boiled away in water.

The food to be steamed is placed in a bamboo steamer, which fits onto the wok (see page 13). Water is boiled in the wok and the steam rises to cook the food in the steamer. The food never actually touches the boiling water.

If you do not have a steamer, see the section on Equipment, page 14, for an alternative. However, a special advantage of the bamboo steamer is that it can be taken directly from the stove to the table because it is decorative as well as functional. It also comes with several layers so that different foods can be steamed at the same time.

A steaming tip: To prevent foods from sticking to the bamboo steamer, line the cooking surfaces with lettuce leaves. Or if you are using a substitute steamer with a rack or a heatproof platter, be sure the rack or platter is well oiled.

Because the water will boil away into steam, you will usually need to replenish the water during the steaming process. Keep a hot water kettle boiling on another burner and when the water is low in the steamer add more from the kettle. (If you use cold water from the tap this will require heating the water to steaming temperatures all over again, which will increase the time and reduce the quality of your steam cooking.)

COOKING EQUIPMENT NEEDED

For the Shrimp-Stuffed Mushrooms in Oyster Sauce: a steamer

For the Won Ton Soup: a 6-quart pot for the won tons, and a 2-quart saucepan for the soup

For the Fish Filet Hunan Style: an electric skillet or deep-fat fryer and a wok or skillet for the sauce

For the Yang Chow Fried Rice: a wok or skillet

For the Cucumber Salad: a mixing bowl

For the Almond Cookies: a cookie sheet

PREPARATION AND COOKING
OF THE MEAL

SHRIMP-STUFFED MUSHROOMS IN OYSTER SAUCE

PREPARATION TIME: 30 MINUTES   CANTON
COOKING TIME: 10 MINUTES

We use dried Chinese mushrooms in this dish. They have a delicate taste that is quite different from fresh or canned mushrooms.
In this case the mushrooms are soaked, then filled with shrimp
and other ingredients, and steamed. The oyster sauce gives them
a special piquant flavor.

16 *dried Chinese mushrooms (2 inches in diameter), soaked in*
    warm water for 30 minutes

FILLING:
½ *pound shrimp, shelled, deveined, and minced*
6   *canned water chestnuts, minced*
3   *tablespoons minced fresh coriander or parsley*
½ *teaspoon salt*
½ *teaspoon sugar*
1   *tablespoon dry sherry*
1   *egg, lightly beaten*

2   *tablespoons oyster sauce*

Lettuce leaves

TO PREPARE:
   1. Rinse mushrooms and discard tough stems.
   2. Combine ingredients for the filling.
   3. Divide the mixture into 16 portions.
   4. Place 1 portion on top of each mushroom.
   5. Spoon a little oyster sauce on the top—about ¼ teaspoon.

TO COOK:
   1. Bring water to a boil in a steamer. (See page 92 for basic
steaming instructions.)

2. Place mushrooms on a steamer rack lined with a layer of lettuce leaves.

3. Steam for 10 minutes.

4. Serve immediately with cocktails or as a first course.

WON TONS

PREPARATION TIME: 1 HOUR AND 30 MINUTES   CANTON
COOKING TIME: 8 MINUTES

Won Tons are quite similar to Italian ravioli. They are noodles with a meat filling that are folded in a special way. They are served boiled and plain, or boiled in soup (see recipe for Won Ton Soup), or deep fried (see recipe for Fried Won Tons). It is easier if you use ready-made won ton skins, but if these are not available use the recipe below. If you want to freeze them, place the won tons uncovered on a tray in the freezer. Do not let them touch or they will stick together. When they are frozen, transfer them to a plastic bag. At a later meal they can be boiled or deep fried without thawing.

WON TON SKINS (*makes about 2 dozen*)

1   *cup all-purpose flour*
¼   *teaspoon salt*
1   *egg, lightly beaten*
¼–½ *cup water*

TO PREPARE:

1. Combine flour and salt.

2. Add egg and gradually add water.

3. Knead with your hands about 10 minutes until dough is soft and elastic.

4. Cover with a damp dish towel and set aside 15 minutes.

5. Roll the dough out on a floured board as thin as you can.

6. Cut into 3-inch squares.

7. Flour each skin so they will not stick together and stack until you are ready to use them. (Skins can be wrapped in foil and refrigerated up to 3 days or frozen until ready to use.)

WON TONS

FILLING:
½ *pound lean, ground pork*
¼ *cup minced onions*
¼ *cup minced celery*
1   *tablespoon soy sauce*
½ *teaspoon dry sherry*
1   *egg*
½ *teaspoon cornstarch*

   24 won ton skins (see preceding recipe)

TO PREPARE:
   Combine all the ingredients for the filling in a large bowl.

TO ASSEMBLE:
   1. Keep skins covered with a damp dish towel while you are
working to prevent them from drying out.
   2. Dampen one side of won ton skin with water.
   3. Place 1 level teaspoon of filling in center of skin and fold
in half.

Won ton

1. Place 1 teaspoon of filling in the center of the skin.

2. Fold in half.

3. Press skin firmly closed around the filling.

4. Fold ends back forming two wings.

5. Moisten one wing and press the two wings together.

4. Press skin firmly closed around the filling.
5. Fold ends back forming two wings.
6. Moisten one wing and press the two wings together.

TO COOK:
1. Bring several quarts of water to a boil.
2. Carefully drop in won tons.
3. Bring to a boil again and cook 8 minutes.
4. Drain.

WON TON SOUP

PREPARATION TIME: 30 MINUTES   CANTON
COOKING TIME: 10 MINUTES

Won Ton Soup is familiar to all who love Chinese food. It is easily made by adding cooked won tons to a broth.

6   *cups canned chicken broth*
½   *teaspoon salt*
¼   *teaspoon white pepper*
6   *dried Chinese mushrooms, soaked in warm water*
    30 minutes

24 *cooked won tons (see preceding recipe)*

¼   *pound fresh spinach, trimmed and shredded*

1   *whole scallion, thinly sliced*

TO PREPARE:
Rinse mushrooms, discard tough stems, and shred.

TO COOK:
1. Combine chicken broth, salt, pepper, and mushrooms.
2. Bring to a boil, cover, and simmer 5 minutes.
3. Add won tons and spinach.
4. Bring to a boil again. (NOTE: If the won tons have been cooked earlier and are cold, simmer in the soup for 5 minutes before serving.)

5. Remove from heat, garnish with scallion.
6. Serve immediately in individual bowls.

FISH FILET HUNAN STYLE

PREPARATION TIME: 30 MINUTES   HUNAN
COOKING TIME: 15 MINUTES

Hunan is a region in China noted for highly seasoned food, particularly spicy fish dishes. In this recipe the fish pieces are fried
in a batter until crisp and then combined with vegetables in a
spicy sauce. The fish can be double-fried as described on page 79
if you like, or kept warm in a low, 200° oven until the sauce is
ready. The sauce can be made ahead, but do not add the cornstarch until just before serving.

1   *pound filet of sole, flounder, or any white fish, cut into*
    2 × 1-inch pieces
Salt and pepper

BATTER:
2   *eggs*
¾   *cup all-purpose flour*
¼   *cup dry sherry*

4   *cups peanut oil for deep frying*

2   *tablespoons peanut oil*

½   *cup lean ground pork*

VEGETABLES:
¼   *cup sweet red or green pepper, diced in ½-inch pieces*
¼   *cup canned bamboo shoots, diced in ½-inch pieces*
4   *dried Chinese mushrooms, soaked in warm water 30 minutes*
1   *whole scallion, minced*
1   *teaspoon minced fresh ginger*
1   *teaspoon minced garlic*

SAUCE:

3   *tablespoons dry sherry*
2   *tablespoons soy sauce*
1   *tablespoon sugar*
3   *tablespoons hoisin sauce*
1   *teaspoon chili paste with garlic*
¾   *cup canned chicken broth*

   1   *tablespoon cornstarch, dissolved in 2 tablespoons*
         cold water

   1   *teaspoon sesame oil (optional)*

TO PREPARE:
   1. Combine ingredients for batter and mix well until smooth.
   2. Sprinkle fish pieces with salt and pepper.
   3. Rinse mushrooms, discard tough stems, dice.

ON THE TRAY:
   Bottle of peanut oil
   Bowl containing fish pieces
   Bowl containing batter
   Cup containing ground pork
   Bowl containing vegetables
   Bowl containing sauce mixed together
   Cup containing dissolved cornstarch
   Bottle of sesame oil

TO COOK:
Step 1:
   1. Heat 4 cups peanut oil to 325° in a deep-fat fryer. (See page 79 for basic deep-frying instructions.)
   2. Dip fish pieces in the batter.
   3. Fry a few pieces at a time about 3 minutes until golden.
   4. Drain on paper towels.
   5. Reserve cooking oil in a covered jar to be used again.

Step 2:
   1. Heat wok or skillet over high heat.
   2. Add 2 tablespoons peanut oil.

3. When hot, add ground pork and stir-fry 1 minute.

4. Add vegetables and stir-fry 1 minute.

5. Add sauce mixture and stir until it boils.

6. Stir dissolved cornstarch, which will have settled, and add.

7. Stir until the sauce thickens, about 1 minute.

8. Remove wok from heat and stir in sesame oil, if desired.

9. Place fried-fish pieces on a serving platter and pour sauce over the top.

10. Serve immediately.

YANG CHOW FRIED RICE

PREPARATION TIME: 30 MINUTES   YANG CHOW
COOKING TIME: 5 MINUTES

Yang Chow Fried Rice is named after the city of its origin, which is well known for its fried rice. It includes fish, meat, and several vegetables. In making fried rice you may add or subtract as many of the ingredients as you like. It is a perfect dish for using leftover cooked chicken, pork, shrimp, etc. This dish can be made completely ahead and then be put into an ovenproof casserole and reheated in the oven at 350° for 30 minutes before serving. For the best results the rice should be cooked the day before so it is thoroughly dry when you fry it.

4   cups cold boiled rice (see pages 65–66)
¼   cup coarsely chopped cooked shrimp
¼   cup diced ham

VEGETABLES:
6   canned water chestnuts, chopped
½   cup bean sprouts or shredded lettuce
¼   cup frozen peas, thawed
6   dried Chinese mushrooms, soaked in warm water 30 minutes
¼   cup whole chopped scallions

2   eggs, scrambled and broken into small pieces

3   tablespoons peanut oil

SAUCE:

2   *tablespoons soy sauce*
1   *tablespoon dry sherry*
1   *teaspoon salt*
¼   *cup canned chicken broth or water*

TO PREPARE:

Rinse mushrooms, discard tough stems, dice.

ON THE TRAY:

Bottle of peanut oil
Bowl containing shrimp, ham, vegetables, and eggs
Bowl containing rice
Cup containing sauce

TO COOK:

1. Heat wok or skillet over high heat.
2. Add 3 tablespoons peanut oil.
3. When oil is hot, add shrimp, ham, vegetables, and eggs and stir-fry 1 minute.
4. Place rice on top of mixture and cover for 1 minute.
5. Stir thoroughly, add sauce, and heat for 3 minutes.
6. Remove from heat and serve immediately.

CUCUMBER SALAD

PREPARATION TIME: 10 MINUTES   PEKING

For this salad you may have the cucumbers sliced and the dressing mixed early in the day, but do not combine until just before serving. Otherwise the soy sauce in the dressing will discolor the white cucumber. The salad can be served at room temperature or chilled.

2   *medium cucumbers*

DRESSING:

1   *tablespoon soy sauce*
1   *teaspoon white rice vinegar*
1   *teaspoon sesame oil*
½   *teaspoon sugar*

TO PREPARE:

1. Peel cucumbers, cut in half lengthwise, and remove seeds.
2. Thinly slice horizontally.
3. Cover and refrigerate.
4. Mix dressing.
5. Combine dressing and cucumbers just before serving.

LICHEE BLACK TEA

PREPARATION TIME: 2 MINUTES
BREWING TIME: 3 MINUTES

See recipe for Green Tea in Menu Lesson 1.

ALMOND COOKIES (*makes about 2 dozen*)

PREPARATION TIME: 30 MINUTES   ALL REGIONS
COOKING TIME: 12 MINUTES

You will notice that this recipe does not specify what kind of shortening to use. The Chinese traditionally use lard but the flavor does not always appeal to American palates, so you may substitute butter, margarine, or vegetable shortening.

1   *cup shortening*
1   *cup sugar*
1   *egg*
2   *tablespoons almond extract*
2½ *cups all-purpose flour*
1½ *teaspoons baking soda*
½   *teaspoon salt*
Blanched whole almonds

TO PREPARE:

1. Cream shortening and sugar in a mixing bowl.
2. Beat egg and add to the mixture along with the almond extract.

3. Sift together flour, baking soda, and salt.

4. Use your hands to blend ingredients together to make a stiff dough.

TO COOK:

1. Preheat oven to 350°.

2. Take a small piece of dough and make a 1-inch ball.

3. Flatten it with your hand and place an almond in the center.

4. Bake on a greased cookie sheet about 12 minutes or until golden on the bottom and still pale on top.

ADVANCE PREPARATION SUGGESTIONS
AND SCHEDULE

A PREVIOUS DAY:

1. Combine the shrimp mixture for the mushrooms.

2. Soak the mushrooms, stuff them, cover and refrigerate up to 2 or 3 days or freeze.

3. Prepare the Won Tons and place on a floured tray. Cover and refrigerate up to 2 or 3 days or freeze.

4. Prepare the Yang Chow Fried Rice. Put it in an ovenproof casserole. Refrigerate up to 2 or 3 days or freeze.

5. Bake the Almond Cookies. Store in a covered container up to 2 weeks.

EARLY ON THE DAY OF THE DINNER:

1. Prepare broth for the soup.

2. Boil Won Tons, add to soup broth, cover and refrigerate.

3. Cut the fish filet into small pieces, dip in batter, and fry. Cover and refrigerate.

4. Prepare sauce/vegetable mixture for Fish Filet Hunan Style but do not add cornstarch until ready to serve. Cover and refrigerate.

5. Slice cucumbers for salad. Cover and refrigerate.

6. Mix dressing for the salad. Cover and refrigerate.

30 MINUTES BEFORE DINNER:

1. Preheat oven to 350°. Heat fried rice 30 minutes. (Heat for 1 hour if frozen.) You may add a little canned chicken broth if it seems dry.

2. Steam mushrooms if you are serving them with cocktails. (Steam for 15 minutes if they are frozen.)

15 MINUTES BEFORE DINNER:

1. Combine cucumbers and dressing.

2. Reheat soup.

3. Reheat sauce/vegetable mixture for the Fish Filet Hunan Style. Thicken with cornstarch.

4. Refry fish filets and combine with sauce.

5 MINUTES BEFORE DINNER:

Start water boiling for tea.

MENU LESSON 5

PUTTING IT ALL TOGETHER
Stir-Frying, Oven-Roasting, Deep Frying, and Steaming

A HEARTY REPAST FOR SIX

Shrimp Toast
Steamed Beef Dumplings
Spicy Soy Dipping Sauce
Roast Pork Strips
Lo Mein
Spicy Green Beans
Lapsang Souchong Tea
Mixed Fruit Compote with Coconut

This selection of dishes will give you additional practice in all four methods of Chinese cooking: Shrimp Toast—deep frying;

Steamed Beef Dumplings—steaming; Roast Pork Strips—oven-roasting; Lo Mein and Spicy Green Beans—stir-frying.

The Shrimp Toast can be served as an appetizer. It is a delicious treat.

Dumplings of all kinds are a large part of the Chinese cuisine. They are often listed as *dim sum* on a restaurant menu and can come in a wide variety of steamed, boiled, or fried versions with many different fillings of meats, vegetables, sweets, etc. There are special restaurants open just for lunch, which serve only dumplings and tea. The dumplings we have in this dinner are steamed, beef-filled dumplings. (See the Index for other dumpling recipes.)

Cantonese Roast Pork Strips are available already cooked in Chinese food stores and are sold by the pound. You will see them hanging with the other cooked meats and poultry, such as roast ducks and spareribs. However, we will make our own.

The Lo Mein dish is made with egg noodles. The Chinese in the northern provinces do not always have rice with their meals. They eat a great amount of wheat, and in this dinner we have dumplings and noodles but no rice.

The green beans are quite spicy and have their origin in Szechuan. We think you'll find them a good contrast to the more bland noodle dish.

Accompanying our dinner will be Lapsang Souchong Tea. It is a hearty black tea with a definite smoky flavor. The dessert is a refreshing fruit combination laced with rum and topped with coconut.

COOKING EQUIPMENT NEEDED

For the Shrimp Toast: a deep-fat fryer or an electric frying pan

For the Steamed Beef Dumplings: a steamer

For the Roast Pork Strips: a roasting pan with a rack

For the Lo Mein: a 6-quart pot for cooking the noodles and a wok or skillet

For the Spicy Green Beans: a 2-quart saucepan for parboiling and a wok or skillet

PREPARATION AND COOKING
OF THE MEAL

SHRIMP TOAST (*makes 24 pieces*)

PREPARATION TIME: 45 MINUTES   CANTON
COOKING TIME: 15 MINUTES

Shrimp Toast is a very popular appetizer made by spreading
bread with a mixture of shrimp, salt pork, egg, and spices and
then frying it upside down. The egg prevents the mixture from
falling off the bread. Use a firm, white sandwich bread and save
the trimmed crusts for making your own bread crumbs in the
blender. It is best to use day-old bread that is slightly stale so it
does not absorb the oil when it is fried. If day-old bread is not
available, spread the bread slices on the kitchen counter to dry
for at least an hour. To save time use frozen shelled and deveined
shrimp. The shrimp toast can be frozen and then reheated when
it is to be served. Reheat in a 425° oven for 6–8 minutes.

6   *thin, white sandwich-bread slices, with crusts trimmed*

SHRIMP MIXTURE:
½   *pound shrimp, finely chopped*
¼   *pound salt pork, finely chopped*
2   *tablespoons minced onion*
½   *teaspoon salt*
1   *egg*
2   *tablespoons chopped parsley*
1   *teaspoon sugar*
½   *teaspoon sesame oil (optional)*
1   *tablespoon cornstarch*

1   *egg, lightly beaten*

Fresh bread crumbs

4   *cups peanut oil*

BEFORE YOU COOK:

1. Spread shrimp mixture thickly over bread, dividing it
equally among the 6 slices.

2. Brush tops with beaten egg.
3. Sprinkle surface with crumbs.
4. Cut each piece into diagonals to make 4 triangles.

TO COOK:

1. Heat 4 cups oil to 375° in a deep-fat fryer. (See page 79 for basic deep-frying instructions.)

2. With a spatula slide each piece of shrimp toast into the hot oil *upside down*. Cook about 4 pieces at a time.

3. Fry about 2 minutes or until the edges of bread are golden brown.

4. Remove with a slotted spoon and drain on paper towels.

5. Keep the cooked shrimp toast in a low, 200° oven while you are frying the remainder.

6. Reserve cooking oil in a covered jar to be reused.

STEAMED BEEF DUMPLINGS

PREPARATION TIME: 1 HOUR AND 30 MINUTES   CANTON
COOKING TIME: 20 MINUTES

Dumplings are popular in China and are made in many shapes with different fillings. In this dinner the dumplings are filled with beef and then steamed. You may substitute ground pork or finely chopped shrimp for the beef. If you prefer, they can be prepared in advance, ready for cooking, and then frozen. It is, of course, easier to use ready-made dumpling skins, but if these are unavailable use the recipe below.

ROUND DUMPLING SKINS (*makes about 2 dozen*)

1   cup all-purpose flour
¼   teaspoon salt
1   egg, lightly beaten
¼–½ cup water

TO PREPARE:

1. Combine flour and salt.
2. Add egg and gradually add water.

3. Knead with your hands about 10 minutes until dough is soft and elastic.

4. Cover with a damp dish towel and set aside 15 minutes.

5. Roll the dough out as thin as you can on a floured board.

6. Cut into 3-inch circles.

7. Flour each skin so they will not stick together and stack until you are ready to use them. (Skins can be wrapped in foil and refrigerated up to 3 days or frozen until ready to use.)

DUMPLINGS

FILLING:

½ *pound lean, ground beef*
1 *teaspoon minced fresh ginger*
1 *tablespoon soy sauce*
1 *tablespoon dry sherry*
4 *canned water chestnuts, minced*
1 *whole scallion, minced*
2 *dried Chinese mushrooms, soaked in warm water 30 minutes*
½ *teaspoon sugar*

  Lettuce leaves

24 *round dumpling skins (see preceding recipe)*

TO PREPARE:

1. Rinse mushrooms, discard tough stems, mince.

2. Mix ingredients for filling together in a large bowl.

TO ASSEMBLE:

1. Keep skins covered with a damp dish towel while you are working to prevent them from drying out.

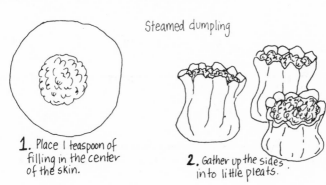

Steamed dumpling

1. Place 1 teaspoon of filling in the center of the skin.

2. Gather up the sides into little pleats.

2. Moisten one side of the skin with water.

3. Place 1 tablespoon of filling in the center of the skin.

4. Gather up the sides into little pleats. (It will have an "hourglass" shape with an open top that shows the meat filling.)

TO COOK:

1. Bring water to a boil in a steamer. (See page 92 for basic steaming instructions.)

2. Place dumplings on a steamer rack lined with lettuce leaves.

3. Steam for 20 minutes.

4. Serve with Spicy Soy Dipping Sauce (see following recipe) or use recipe for Hot Mustard Sauce.

SPICY SOY DIPPING SAUCE

PREPARATION TIME: 5 MINUTES   PEKING

    3   *tablespoons soy sauce*
    3   *tablespoons white rice vinegar*
    ½   *teaspoon sesame oil*
    ½   *teaspoon hot oil*

    1   *whole scallion, minced*

TO PREPARE:

1. Combine sauce ingredients and stir.

2. Sprinkle with scallion.

3. Serve in a separate dish.

ROAST PORK STRIPS

MARINATING TIME: 3 HOURS OR OVERNIGHT   CANTON
PREPARATION TIME: 15 MINUTES
COOKING TIME: 1 HOUR

Cantonese Roast Pork Strips are delicious and they can be used in a number of different ways. In this menu we will serve the meat cut up into small portions to be dipped into either the Hot Mustard Sauce, the Duck Sauce, or both. In other recipes the cooked pork can be combined with vegetables and stir-fried (see recipe for Roast Pork with Vegetables) or served with cooked rice or noodles. The Chinese often color the roast pork with red 'dye but we prefer not to. The pork strips can be cooked in advance and then wrapped tightly in foil and refrigerated or frozen until you are ready to use.

2   *pounds lean pork loin, cut into 1 × 2 × 6-inch strips*

MARINADE:

1   *whole scallion, minced*
1   *teaspoon minced fresh ginger*
½   *teaspoon minced garlic*
1   *tablespoon catsup*
1   *tablespoon hoisin sauce*
½   *teaspoon 5-spice powder*
2   *tablespoons dry sherry*
2   *tablespoons soy sauce*
1   *tablespoon brown sugar*
1   *teaspoon salt*
¼   *teaspoon black pepper*

     Honey

TO PREPARE:

1. Mix ingredients for the marinade in a large bowl.

2. Add pork strips and marinate at least 3 hours at room temperature or overnight in the refrigerator.

3. Turn meat occasionally.

TO COOK:

1. Use a roasting pan with a rack.

2. Pour 2 cups water into the bottom of the pan.

3. Place rack with meat on it in the pan. *Do not let the meat touch the water.* Reserve the marinade.

4. Preheat oven to 400°.

5. Cook meat 50 minutes, turning and basting frequently.

6. Remove from oven and brush on honey.

7. Slice into ½-inch pieces and serve with Hot Mustard and Duck Sauces.

LO MEIN

PREPARATION TIME: 30 MINUTES   CANTON
COOKING TIME: 6 MINUTES

Lo Mein is a noodle dish. In this dinner we combine the noodles with vegetables. The noodles are boiled separately ahead of time, the vegetables are stir-fried, and then the two are tossed together. When boiling the noodles be sure not to overcook them. They should be soft outside but still firm in the center. This dish, like fried rice, allows you to be creative. Just let your imagination and the leftovers in your refrigerator be your guide. Lo Mein may be made ahead and reheated.

½ pound fresh Chinese egg noodles

VEGETABLES:
4   *whole scallions, cut into 1-inch pieces and shredded*
4   *dried Chinese mushrooms, soaked in warm water 30 minutes*
     (Reserve soaking liquid.)
2   *cups iceberg lettuce, shredded*

    2   *tablespoons peanut oil*

SAUCE:
3   *tablespoons soy sauce*
½   *teaspoon salt*
1   *teaspoon sugar*
½   *cup mushroom soaking liquid*

TO PREPARE:
   1. Rinse mushrooms, discard tough stems, shred.
   2. Bring 6 quarts of water to a boil, add noodles, and cook 2 minutes. Drain, rinse in cold water, and mix with 2 tablespoons peanut oil.

ON THE TRAY:
   Bottle of peanut oil
   Bowl containing vegetables
   Cup containing sauce mixed together
   Bowl containing cooked noodles

TO COOK:

1. Heat wok or skillet over high heat.
2. Add 2 tablespoons peanut oil.
3. When oil is hot add vegetables and stir-fry 2 minutes.
4. Add sauce and stir-fry 1 minute.
5. Toss in cooked noodles and stir about 3 minutes until blended and heated through.
6. Remove from heat and serve immediately.

SPICY GREEN BEANS

PREPARATION TIME: 15 MINUTES   SZECHUAN
COOKING TIME: 6 MINUTES

This dish uses fresh, whole green beans that have been parboiled for 3 minutes before they are stir-fried with the other ingredients. They should be prepared just before serving to preserve the crunchy texture of the beans.

½   *pound fresh green beans, ends trimmed*
1   *tablespoon peanut oil*
3   *dried red chili peppers, cut in half*

PORK AND SHRIMP MIXTURE:
¼   *cup lean, ground pork*
10 *dried shrimp, soaked in warm water 30 minutes, then minced*
1   *teaspoon minced fresh ginger*
½   *teaspoon minced garlic*

SAUCE:
1   *teaspoon sugar*
2   *tablespoons dry sherry*
½   *teaspoon salt*
2   *tablespoons soy sauce*

   1   *teaspoon cornstarch, dissolved in 2 tablespoons*
       cold water

   1   *teaspoon sesame oil (optional)*

TO PREPARE:

1. Combine pork and shrimp mixture and mix well.

2. Bring 1 quart of water to a boil, add green beans, and boil 3 minutes. Drain, rinse under cold water.

ON THE TRAY:

Bottle of peanut oil
Cup containing red peppers
Bowl containing pork and shrimp mixture
Bowl containing green beans
Cup containing sauce mixed together
Cup containing dissolved cornstarch
Bottle of sesame oil

TO COOK:

1. Heat wok or skillet over high heat.

2. When hot add 1 tablespoon peanut oil.

3. When oil is hot add red peppers and stir-fry about 30 seconds until peppers turn black.

4. Add pork and shrimp mixture and stir-fry 1 minute or until the pork loses its pink color.

5. Add green beans and stir.

6. Add sauce and stir-fry 1 minute.

7. Stir dissolved cornstarch, which will have settled, and add.

8. Stir until sauce is thickened, about 1 minute.

9. Remove from heat and stir in sesame oil, if desired. Serve immediately.

LAPSANG SOUCHONG TEA

PREPARATION TIME: 2 MINUTES
BREWING TIME: 3 MINUTES

See recipe for Green Tea in Menu Lesson 1.

MIXED FRUIT COMPOTE WITH COCONUT

PREPARATION TIME: 10 MINUTES
CHILLING TIME: 3 HOURS

1   *package frozen mixed fruit*
1   *package frozen melon balls*
1   *banana, sliced*
½   *cup rum*
Shredded coconut

1. Combine fruits and rum. Chill at least 3 hours.
2. To serve, spoon into individual dishes and top with coconut.

ADVANCE PREPARATION SUGGESTIONS
AND SCHEDULE

A PREVIOUS DAY:

1. Marinate and roast the pork strips. Wrap in foil and refrigerate up to 3 days or freeze.

2. Prepare and fry the Shrimp Toast. Wrap tightly in foil and
refrigerate up to 3 days or freeze.

3. Prepare and assemble dumplings. Wrap and refrigerate up
to 3 days or freeze. Prepare dipping sauce; refrigerate.

EARLY ON THE DAY OF THE DINNER:

1. Prepare the Lo Mein. Put in an ovenproof casserole and
refrigerate.

2. Trim green beans and parboil. Cover and refrigerate.

3. Mix sauce for green beans but do not add cornstarch until
just before serving. Cover and refrigerate.

4. Prepare shrimp and pork mixture for the green beans.
Cover and refrigerate.

5. Combine fruits and rum for dessert. Chill.

40 MINUTES BEFORE DINNER:

Preheat oven to 425° and reheat Shrimp Toast for 3–5 minutes (8 minutes if frozen). Serve with cocktails.

30 MINUTES BEFORE DINNER:

Reduce oven to 350° and reheat Lo Mein.

20 MINUTES BEFORE DINNER:

Start the dumplings steaming (30 minutes if they are frozen).

10 MINUTES BEFORE DINNER:

Reheat Roast Pork Strips in 350° oven (30 minutes if they
are frozen).

5 MINUTES BEFORE DINNER:

1. Stir-fry the green beans.

2. Start water boiling for tea.

MENU LESSON 6

THE GRAND FINALE

A BANQUET FOR EIGHT

COLD DISHES:
Tea Eggs
Sliced Fragrant Beef
Spicy Pickled Salad

Peking Duck
Mandarin Pancakes
Scallion Brushes and Peking Sauce
Hot and Sour Soup
Spicy Kung Pao Jumbo Shrimp
Broccoli with Dried Mushrooms
Boiled Rice
Jasmine Tea
Peking Honey Bananas

We hope you've now gained enough confidence in your Chinese cooking skills to tackle a banquet for eight people. A banquet traditionally begins with cold platters already on the table when the guests are seated. We will serve three different cold dishes, all made well in advance of dinner.

Roasted meat or poultry is generally on a banquet menu. We will have a simplified version of Peking Duck that you can cook quite easily at home. Serve it with Mandarin Pancakes, a Peking Sauce, and Scallion Brushes, just as it is served in restaurants.

Soup is served midway in the dinner to offer a change of pace and a rest before continuing with the remaining dishes. Hot and Sour Soup is an unusual and delicious soup that combines some exotic vegetables that we have not used before in the course.

Spicy Kung Pao Jumbo Shrimp are mildly spicy and lightly sweet and are complemented by the Broccoli with Dried Mushrooms.

Jasmine Tea is a black tea with dried flower blossoms added and is very aromatic.

Peking Honey Bananas are a favorite at the Mandarin Inn. They are one of the most special of the Chinese sweets. Batter-fried chunks of banana are dipped in a caramel sauce and then into ice water, to give them a crisp outer coating.

COOKING EQUIPMENT NEEDED

For the Tea Eggs: a 2-quart saucepan

For the Sliced Fragrant Beef: a 4-quart covered casserole

For the Spicy Pickled Salad: a large mixing bowl

For the Peking Duck: a roasting pan with a rack

For the Mandarin Pancakes: a rolling pin, a 3-inch cookie cutter, a skillet, and a steamer for reheating

For the Peking Sauce: a 1-quart saucepan

For the Hot and Sour Soup: a 2-quart saucepan

For the Spicy Kung Pao Jumbo Shrimp: a wok or skillet and an electric frying pan or a deep-fat fryer

For the Broccoli with Dried Mushrooms: a wok or skillet and a 4-quart saucepan for parboiling

For the Peking Honey Bananas: an electric frying pan or deep-fat fryer and a 2-quart saucepan for the caramel coating

For the rice: a 2-quart saucepan

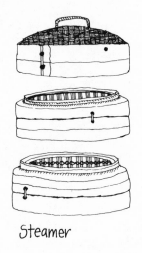

Steamer

PREPARATION AND COOKING
OF THE MEAL

TEA EGGS

PREPARATION TIME: 5 MINUTES   NINGPO
COOKING TIME: 2 HOURS
CHILLING TIME: 3 HOURS

Tea Eggs are pleasing both to the palate and to the eye. Their shells are cracked, then they are cooked in tea and spices so that the entire surface of the egg has a marbled effect.

8 *eggs*

¼ *cup black tea*
3 *tablespoons soy sauce*
1 *tablespoon salt*
1 *teaspoon star anise*

TO COOK:

Step 1:

1. Place eggs in a saucepan and cover with cold water.
2. Bring to a boil slowly and simmer 30 minutes.
3. Drain and rinse in cold water.
4. When cool enough to handle roll eggs on kitchen counter top, pressing firmly to crack the shells, but do not peel. (Be careful not to break off any pieces of the shell. The eggs should have an all-over crackled appearance.)

Step 2:

1. Place eggs in a saucepan, cover with water, and add remaining ingredients.
2. Bring to a boil, cover, and simmer 1½ hours. The crackled surface of the eggs will absorb the dark tea liquid, giving the eggs a marbled appearance.
3. Remove from heat and allow eggs to cool in liquid before refrigerating.
4. Do not peel until just before serving.
5. When ready to serve, peel and cut each egg into 4 wedges.

SLICED FRAGRANT BEEF

PREPARATION TIME: 10 MINUTES   SHANGHAI
COOKING TIME: 2 HOURS
CHILLING TIME: 4 HOURS OR OVERNIGHT

In this dish the beef has been slowly simmered with flavorings and spices until it is very tender. The simmering liquid is called a master sauce and can be reserved in the refrigerator to be used again for this recipe. After the meat is cooked it is chilled before serving.

2   *pounds boneless beef shin or beef chuck*

MASTER SAUCE:
2   *cups water*
1   *teaspoon star anise*
3   *tablespoons dry sherry*
3   *tablespoons soy sauce*
3   *slices fresh ginger, about 1 inch in diameter and ⅛ inch thick*
3   *cloves garlic*
1   *teaspoon salt*
1   *teaspoon sugar*

TO COOK:
1. Combine all the ingredients in a large covered casserole and bring to a boil.
2. Reduce heat and simmer for 2 hours.
3. Remove meat from liquid, wrap in foil, and refrigerate.
4. Serve the beef thinly sliced on a platter.

SPICY PICKLED SALAD

PREPARATION TIME: 20 MINUTES   SZECHUAN
MARINATING TIME: 3 DAYS

Spicy Pickled Salad is a specialty of the Mandarin Inn. These tangy tidbits are put on the table for guests to nibble while they study the menu. The salad is a combination of cabbage, carrots, and green peppers marinated in a dressing of vinegar, sugar, spices, and dried chili peppers to give it a spicy flavor.

The cabbage used is the regular round head of cabbage available in all supermarkets. The recipe calls for crushing the garlic and the ginger. Do this by pressing down hard with the flat side of the cleaver. This will release their juices.

It is important to marinate the vegetables for 3 full days so they absorb the flavorings. After the 3 days, remove the red peppers, garlic, and ginger. Store in a covered jar in the refrigerator. It will keep up to 2 weeks.

VEGETABLES:

1 *small head of cabbage, cut into 1-inch squares*
2 *carrots, cut into ½-inch diagonal slices*
2 *green peppers, cut into 1-inch squares*

MARINADE:

1 *cup white rice vinegar*
1 *cup sugar*
2 *2-inch cubes fresh ginger, crushed*
8 *garlic cloves, crushed*
8 *dried red chili peppers, cut in half*
1 *quart water*

TO PREPARE:

1. Place vegetables in a 4-quart mixing bowl.

2. Combine marinade and pour over the vegetables.

3. Place a smaller plate on top of the vegetables and press down.

4. Refrigerate for 3 days, turning the vegetables occasionally in the marinade.

5. Remove the red peppers, garlic, and ginger and drain before serving.

PEKING DUCK

PREPARATION TIME: 14 HOURS   PEKING
COOKING TIME: 1 HOUR AND 15 MINUTES

Peking Duck has always seemed impossibly complicated to make at home because of the elaborate preparation that is required. To have the skin be cooked properly, crisp and dry with no trace of fat, it is necessary to separate the skin of the duck from the fat to enable its grease to be released in cooking. This is traditionally done by inserting a tube between the skin and fat of the duck and blowing to loosen the skin. Needless to say, this is a long and exhausting procedure. However, Chef Alex Wong of the Mandarin Inn has devised a simple alternative that produces a great Peking duck and even makes it fun to do. You begin by preparing the duck the day before you plan to cook it. It is dipped in fresh boiling water several times. (Use fresh water each time because otherwise grease will accumulate in it.) This process frees the skin from the fat. The duck is then hung in a cool place in the kitchen (look for a place in which it can hang freely) for at least 12 hours with a dish under it to collect the dripping fat. The remainder of the fat will be released during the roasting so the duck will be moist but not fatty and the skin will be crisp.

1   4–5-pound fresh or frozen duckling, thawed

Boiling water to cover (Use fresh water each time.)

1   cup honey

16   mandarin pancakes, see pages 124–25

16   scallion brushes, see page 126

Peking sauce, see page 126

TO PREPARE:

1. Tie a string (or use a heavy "S" hook) around the neck or wing of the duck to facilitate dunking it in and out of the boiling water.

2. Bring water to a boil in a pot large enough to submerge the duck.

3. Plunge duck into the boiling water and leave for 30 seconds.

4. Hang duck up to dry for 1 hour in a cool place in the kitchen with a dish under it to collect the fat.

5. Bring fresh water to a boil a second time and submerge duck 30 seconds.

6. Hang duck up to dry for 1 hour as described above.

7. Bring fresh water to a boil a third time and add 1 cup of honey, stir, and bring to a boil again.

8. Submerge duck for 30 seconds.

9. Hang duck up to dry for 12 hours as described above.

TO COOK:

1. Preheat oven to 450°.

2. Place duck, breast down, on a rack in a dry roasting pan.

3. Roast for 30 minutes.

4. Turn duck over and roast for 30 minutes more. (Be careful not to break the skin when you turn it.)

5. Turn off the oven heat.

6. Leave duck in the oven 15 minutes more.

7. Remove and serve.

TO SERVE:

1. Carve the duck, taking care to slice the crispy skin separately from the meat.

2. Arrange the pancakes, the duck meat and the skin, and the Scallion Brushes on a large platter. Serve the Peking Sauce in a separate bowl.

3. Each guest will serve himself by taking a pancake, painting on some Peking Sauce with the Scallion Brush, then putting on a piece of skin, a piece of meat, and the Scallion Brush. The pancake is then rolled up and eaten with the fingers.

MANDARIN PANCAKES (*makes about 16 pancakes*)

PREPARATION TIME: 45 MINUTES   PEKING
COOKING TIME: 15 MINUTES

Mandarin Pancakes, sometimes called doilies, are also served with Mu Shu Pork (see recipe). The pancakes can be made several days ahead, wrapped well and refrigerated, or they may be frozen. Reheat by steaming 10 to 15 minutes.

2   *cups all-purpose flour*
1   *cup boiling water*
Sesame oil

TO PREPARE:

1. Place flour in a mixing bowl.

2. Gradually stir in boiling water, mixing with a wooden spoon.

3. When cool enough to handle, knead with your hands until it is smooth and elastic, adding a little more flour if necessary.

4. Cover dough with a damp dish towel and let it rest for 30 minutes.

5. Roll dough out on a lightly floured surface to a ¼-inch thickness.

6. Use a 3-inch round cookie cutter to cut the dough, re-rolling it until all of the dough has been used.

7. Smear sesame oil over one side of each 3-inch circle of dough.

8. Put two circles together with the sesame-oiled sides touching.

9. Now roll out the double circles until they are about 6 inches in diameter, turning them as you roll so they keep a round shape.

10. Cover the pancakes with a damp towel until you are ready to cook them.

TO COOK:

1. Use an ungreased heavy skillet over low heat and roast one side of the pancake until it bubbles slightly (about 1 minute).

2. Do *not* brown.

3. Turn over and roast the other side.

4. Remove from the skillet and when cool enough to handle pull the two pancakes apart.

5. Wrap the batch of pancakes in foil and refrigerate.

TO REHEAT:

1. Fold each pancake into quarters and place in a steamer. (See page 92 for basic steaming instructions.)

2. Steam for 5 minutes.

NOTE: Another method is to place folded pancakes on top of rice that has just been cooked. The heat and steam from the rice will reheat them.

SCALLION BRUSHES

PREPARATION TIME: 10 MINUTES   PEKING
CHILLING TIME: 1 HOUR

The scallions are specially cut so they curl up at both ends and are actually used as brushes to spread the Peking Sauce over the Mandarin Pancakes. They are then tucked into the pancakes and eaten with the duck.

16 scallions

TO PREPARE:

1. Cut scallions about 3 to 4 inches long from the root end.
2. With a sharp knife make several vertical cuts about ½ inch long in both ends of the scallion.
3. Place in a bowl of ice water in the refrigerator 1 hour or longer. Both ends will curl so that the scallions resemble brushes. Serve on a platter with the Mandarin Pancakes.

PEKING SAUCE

PREPARATION TIME: 3 MINUTES   PEKING
COOKING TIME: 5 MINUTES

This sauce is spread over the Mandarin Pancake before adding the meat and scallion. It gives the Peking Duck its special flavor.

1   cup hoisin sauce
⅓ cup canned chicken broth
1   tablespoon sesame oil
1   tablespoon soy sauce

TO COOK:

1. Heat ingredients together in a small saucepan.
2. Serve warm in a bowl.

HOT AND SOUR SOUP

PREPARATION TIME: 30 MINUTES   PEKING
COOKING TIME: 12 MINUTES

This fabulous soup is very popular. It combines vinegar and white pepper to give it an interesting and unusual flavor. The soup contains some exotic ingredients that can be obtained either by mail or in a Chinatown. Tree ears are a kind of dried fungus and tiger lily buds are the dried blossoms of the tiger lily. Both must be soaked before using. Note that all the ingredients are shredded to give a uniform appearance to the soup. The scallion is used as a garnish.

¼ cup shredded pork (See page 17 for instructions in shredding.)

6 cups canned chicken broth

MARINADE:

1 teaspoon dry sherry
1 teaspoon cornstarch

VEGETABLES:

2 tablespoons tree ears, soaked in warm water 30 minutes
4 dried Chinese mushrooms, soaked in warm water 30 minutes
8 dried tiger lily buds, soaked in warm water 30 minutes

SEASONINGS:

4 tablespoons soy sauce
½ teaspoon sugar
½ teaspoon salt
½ teaspoon white pepper
3 tablespoons white rice vinegar

3 tablespoons cornstarch, dissolved in 3 tablespoons cold water

1 egg, lightly beaten

1 tablespoon sesame oil (optional)

1 whole scallion, thinly sliced

TO PREPARE:

1. Mix marinade until it is smooth, add pork, and marinate 30 minutes.

2. Rinse soaked tree ears thoroughly to remove any sand, then shred.

3. Rinse mushrooms, discard tough stems, and shred.

4. Remove the hard stem end of the tiger lilies and pull each blossom apart into two or three shreds.

ON THE TRAY:

Chicken broth

Bowl containing vegetables and marinated pork

Cup containing seasonings

Cup containing dissolved cornstarch

Cup containing egg

Bottle of sesame oil

Cup containing scallion

TO COOK:

1. Bring chicken broth to a boil in a saucepan.

2. Add pork and vegetables and bring to a boil again.

3. Cover and simmer 10 minutes.

4. Add seasonings and stir.

5. Stir dissolved cornstarch, which will have settled, and add.

6. Stir soup until thickened, about 1 minute.

7. With a chopstick or a wooden spoon gently stir the soup as you slowly pour in the egg. The egg will form delicate shreds in the soup.

8. Remove from heat and stir in sesame oil, if desired.

9. Garnish with scallion and serve immediately in individual bowls.

SPICY KUNG PAO JUMBO SHRIMP

PREPARATION TIME: 30 MINUTES   SZECHUAN
MARINATING TIME: 30 MINUTES
COOKING TIME: 10 MINUTES

As we have said, Szechuan food is noted for its use of hot chili peppers to make the food especially spicy. You may regulate the "hotness" by using fewer or more peppers. The 4 peppers called for in this recipe will make it mildly hot.

In this dish the shrimp are deep fried but are not particularly crispy. The shrimp are combined with the sauce just before serving.

1   *pound large shrimp, shelled and deveined (about 24 shrimp)*

MARINADE:
1   *egg*
3   *tablespoons cornstarch*

4   *cups peanut oil for deep frying*

3   *tablespoons peanut oil*

SEASONINGS:
3   *whole scallions, minced*
1   *teaspoon minced fresh ginger*
1   *teaspoon minced garlic*
4   *whole dried chili peppers, cut in half*

SAUCE:
2   *tablespoons sugar*
1   *tablespoon dry sherry*
2   *tablespoons white rice vinegar*
2   *tablespoons water*

1   *tablespoon sesame oil (optional)*

TO PREPARE:

1. Combine the ingredients for the marinade in a bowl and mix until smooth.

2. Add shrimp and marinate 30 minutes.

ON THE TRAY:
Bottle of peanut oil
Bowl of marinated shrimp
Bowl containing seasonings
Cup containing sauce mixed together
Sesame oil

TO COOK:
Step 1:
1. Heat 4 cups peanut oil to 350° in a deep-fat fryer. (See page 79 for basic deep-frying instructions.)
2. Fry shrimp about 2 minutes until almost done.
3. Drain on paper towels.
4. Reserve cooking oil in a covered jar to be used again.

Step 2:
1. Heat wok or skillet over high heat.
2. Add 3 tablespoons peanut oil.
3. When wok is hot add seasonings and stir-fry 1 minute.
4. Add sauce and stir about 1 minute until boiling.
5. Add fried shrimp and stir about 1 minute until heated through.
6. Remove wok from heat and stir in sesame oil, if desired.
7. Serve immediately.

BROCCOLI WITH DRIED MUSHROOMS

PREPARATION TIME: 30 MINUTES   CANTON
COOKING TIME: 5 MINUTES

This is a delicious way to prepare broccoli. The mushrooms add an interesting flavor. The broccoli is briefly parboiled just to tenderize it. You use only the broccoli flowers for this recipe, but see the recipe for Broccoli Stem Salad that uses the stems.

1   *bunch broccoli, flowers only*

8   *dried Chinese mushrooms, soaked in warm water*
    30 minutes (Reserve soaking liquid.)

3   *tablespoons peanut oil*

SAUCE:

2   tablespoons soy sauce
2   teaspoons dry sherry
1   teaspoon sugar
½   teaspoon salt
½   cup reserved mushroom liquid

    1   tablespoon cornstarch, dissolved in 2 tablespoons
       cold water

TO PREPARE:

    1. Bring 3 quarts of water to a boil, add broccoli, and boil for 3 minutes. Drain and rinse in cold water.

    2. Rinse mushrooms, discard tough stems, cut into quarters.

ON THE TRAY:

    Bottle of peanut oil
    Bowl containing broccoli
    Cup containing mushrooms
    Cup containing sauce mixed together
    Cup containing dissolved cornstarch

TO COOK:

    1. Heat wok or skillet over high heat.
    2. Add 3 tablespoons peanut oil.
    3. When wok is hot add the broccoli and stir-fry 1 minute.
    4. Add mushrooms and stir.
    5. Add sauce and stir until it boils.
    6. Stir dissolved cornstarch, which will have settled, and add.
    7. Stir until sauce is thickened, about 1 minute.
    8. Remove from heat and serve immediately.

BOILED RICE

PREPARATION TIME: 2 MINUTES
COOKING TIME: 40 MINUTES

    See Menu Lesson 1.

JASMINE TEA

PREPARATION TIME: 2 MINUTES
BREWING TIME: 3 MINUTES

See recipe for Green Tea in Menu Lesson 1.

PEKING HONEY BANANAS

PREPARATION TIME: 10 MINUTES   PEKING
COOKING TIME: 10 MINUTES

This dessert is absolutely delicious but it does require last-minute work. The bananas are dipped in batter and deep fried, then dipped into a caramelized syrup and plunged into ice water to harden the syrup. It is not difficult but timing is very important, so have everything ready before you begin cooking.

3   *bananas, cut into 1-inch slices*

BATTER:
½   *cup all-purpose flour*
½   *cup cornstarch*
½   *teaspoon salt*
2   *teaspoons baking powder*
1   *cup water*

4   *cups peanut oil for deep frying*

SYRUP:
1   *cup sugar*
½   *cup water*
4   *tablespoons peanut oil*

1   *bowl ice water*

TO PREPARE:
1. Combine ingredients for batter and mix until smooth.
2. Combine ingredients for syrup in a small saucepan.

TO COOK:

Step 1:

    1. Heat 4 cups peanut oil to 375° in a deep-fat fryer. (See page 79 for basic deep-frying instructions.)

    2. Dip bananas in batter and deep fry about 3 minutes until crisp and golden.

    3. Drain on paper towels.

    4. Reserve cooking oil in a covered jar to be used again.

Step 2:

    Boil ingredients for syrup until the water evaporates and the sugar reaches the hard-crack stage. (Test by putting a few drops of syrup in ice water. When the syrup hardens it is ready.)

TO SERVE:

    1. Dip the hot fried bananas into the caramel syrup.

    2. Place on a well-oiled plate.

    3. Plunge the bananas into ice water for 30 seconds.

    4. Serve immediately in individual bowls.

ADVANCE PREPARATION SUGGESTIONS
AND SCHEDULE

THREE DAYS BEFORE:

Prepare the Spicy Pickled Salad.

A PREVIOUS DAY:

1. Prepare the Sliced Fragrant Beef, wrap in foil, and refrigerate up to 3 days. Store master sauce in a covered container in the freezer.

2. Prepare Tea Eggs. Store with shells on in the refrigerator up to 3 days.

3. Make the Mandarin Pancakes. Wrap in foil and refrigerate up to 3 days or freeze. Defrost before reheating.

THE DAY BEFORE:

1. Shell and devein shrimp. Put in marinade, cover, and refrigerate.

2. Prepare Peking Duck. Hang in a cool place for 12 hours.

3. Make Scallion Brushes. Put in ice water in the refrigerator.

4. Prepare Peking Sauce. Cover and refrigerate.

EARLY ON THE DAY OF THE DINNER:

1. Soak tree ears, mushrooms, and tiger lily buds 30 minutes. Drain and shred. Put in a covered bowl and refrigerate.

2. Mix seasonings for the soup, cover, and refrigerate.

3. Shred pork for soup and combine with marinade. Cover and refrigerate. Remember pork is easier to shred if it is slightly frozen.

4. Prepare vegetables for shrimp dish, cover, and refrigerate.

5. Prepare sauce for shrimp dish, cover, and refrigerate.

5a. Fry the shrimp until almost done, cover, and refrigerate.

6. Parboil broccoli, cover, and refrigerate.

7. Prepare mushrooms for broccoli, cover, and refrigerate.

8. Mix sauce for broccoli but do not add cornstarch until just before serving. Cover and refrigerate.

9. Prepare batter for bananas. Deep fry them, cover, and refrigerate.

10. Drain the Spicy Pickled Salad, put in a covered serving bowl, and refrigerate.

1 HOUR AND 15 MINUTES BEFORE DINNER:
Preheat oven to 400° and roast the duck.

40 MINUTES BEFORE DINNER:
Start the rice.

20 MINUTES BEFORE DINNER:
1. Place pancakes, folded in quarters, on top of the rice and replace cover.
2. Prepare the soup.
3. Combine ingredients for banana syrup in a saucepan.

DINNER:
1. Guests are seated and eat cold dishes.
2. Peking Duck is served with pancakes, scallions, and sauce.
3. Soup is served.

DURING DINNER:
1. Stir-fry broccoli.
2. Reheat sauce for Spicy Kung Pao Jumbo Shrimp, add shrimp, and stir until hot.
3. Serve broccoli, shrimp, and rice.

AFTER DINNER:
1. Cook syrup for the bananas.
2. Briefly refry the bananas.
3. Combine bananas and syrup and serve at the table.

MORE MENUS

The first six Chinese menu lessons should serve to prepare you and whet your appetite for more. You have learned the basic cooking methods, tried many of the standard Chinese ingredients, seen what dishes go together. And you have discovered how easy it is to make dishes from one of the world's finest cuisines.

The following section brings you a number of additional menus planned variously for two, four, or six people. Special care has been taken to combine dishes that offer a good balance of meats, seafood, and vegetables, a variety of tastes, a blending of regional specialties, and a chance to use the several different Chinese cooking methods. The menus offer a reasonable proportion of dishes that can be made ahead so that everything does not have to be done in a last-minute flurry.

Remember, though, that these menu plans are just suggestions. You should, of course, feel free to substitute dishes from the recipe section beginning on page 215 or from other menus, or to drop or add dishes if your circumstances call for it. Just try, as we have, to maintain a reasonable balance in the planning of your menu revisions.

We have not included tea or desserts in these menu plans, nor have we repeated the recipe for boiled rice that appears on pages 65–66. Follow the instructions on page 66 for preparing tea. If you want a dessert, you can use one of the recipes included in the first six menus or serve ice cream or fruit. If you do have a dessert, you may want to drop one of the other dishes in the menu if the combination seems to be too much.

MENU 7

SERVES TWO

Beef with Snow Peas and Water Chestnuts
Kung Pao Chicken with Peanuts
Boiled Rice

Both dishes in the following menu are stir-fried but the chicken
dish can be made ahead. It can successfully be reheated at the
last minute if you do not add the peanuts until the very end.
The peanuts tend to get soggy if reheated.

BEEF WITH SNOW PEAS AND WATER CHESTNUTS

PREPARATION TIME: 20 MINUTES   CANTON
MARINATING TIME: 30 MINUTES
COOKING TIME: 5 MINUTES

> ½ pound flank steak, thinly sliced across the grain, ¼ inch
>   thick × 2 inches long

MARINADE:
1   teaspoon dry sherry
1   egg
¼   teaspoon salt
1   tablespoon peanut oil

2   tablespoons peanut oil

1   tablespoon peanut oil

VEGETABLES:
1   cup fresh or frozen snow peas, stems and strings removed
12   canned water chestnuts, sliced
8   dried Chinese mushrooms, soaked in warm water 30 minutes

SAUCE:
2   tablespoons soy sauce
1   tablespoon dry sherry
1   teaspoon sugar
½   cup canned chicken broth

1   tablespoon cornstarch, dissolved in 2 tablespoons
     cold water

TO PREPARE:
Combine ingredients for marinade and mix until smooth.
Add beef slices and set aside 30 minutes.

Bring 1 quart of water to a boil, add snow peas, stir, and
drain. Rinse in cold water.

Rinse mushrooms, discard tough stems, and slice.

ON THE TRAY:
Bottle of peanut oil

Bowl containing marinated beef slices
Bowl containing vegetables
Bowl containing sauce
Cup containing dissolved cornstarch

TO COOK:

To a heated wok add 2 tablespoons peanut oil. When oil is
hot, add marinated beef and stir-fry 2 minutes until beef loses its
pink color. Remove meat from wok and set aside in a bowl.

In the same wok heat 1 tablespoon peanut oil. Add vegetables
and stir-fry 1 minute. Add sauce and stir. When sauce comes to
a boil, return beef to wok and stir 1 minute. Add dissolved
cornstarch and stir about 1 minute until thickened. Remove from
heat and serve immediately.

KUNG PAO CHICKEN WITH PEANUTS

PREPARATION TIME: 20 MINUTES   SZECHUAN
MARINATING TIME: 30 MINUTES
COOKING TIME: 5 MINUTES

2   *whole chicken breasts, boned, skinned, and cut into*
    ½-inch cubes

MARINADE:
1   *egg*
½   *teaspoon salt*
1   *tablespoon cornstarch*
2   *teaspoons peanut oil*

    ¼   *cup peanut oil*

    2   *tablespoons peanut oil*

    4   *whole dried chili peppers, cut in half*

VEGETABLES:
1   *teaspoon minced fresh ginger*
1   *teaspoon minced garlic*
1   *whole scallion, minced*
5   *whole scallions, cut into ½-inch pieces*

SAUCE:

½ teaspoon chili paste with garlic
3 tablespoons water
1 tablespoon dry sherry
1 teaspoon sugar
2 tablespoons soy sauce

  ½ cup unsalted roasted peanuts

  1 teaspoon sesame oil (optional)

TO PREPARE:

Combine ingredients for marinade and mix until smooth. Add chicken and set aside for 30 minutes.

ON THE TRAY:

Bottle of peanut oil
Bowl containing chicken in marinade
Cup containing dried peppers
Cup containing vegetables
Cup containing sauce
Cup containing peanuts
Bottle of sesame oil

TO COOK:

To a heated wok add ¼ cup peanut oil. When oil is hot add marinated chicken and stir-fry about 2 minutes until it loses its pink color. Remove chicken and set aside in a bowl.

In the same wok heat 2 tablespoons of peanut oil. Add peppers and stir-fry about 30 seconds until they turn black. Add vegetables and stir-fry 30 seconds. Add sauce and stir until it comes to a boil. Return chicken to wok and stir-fry 1 minute to heat through. Add peanuts and stir-fry 1 minute. Remove from heat, stir in sesame oil, if desired, and serve immediately.

MENU 8

SERVES TWO

Shrimp with Lobster Sauce
Stir-Fried Spinach
Boiled Rice

Lobster Sauce does not contain lobster meat, as many people mistakenly believe. Its name derives from a sauce traditionally used over lobster. You cook the shrimp and the sauce separately and combine them just before serving.

Stir-Fried Spinach is cooked quickly at the last minute, just until the spinach is wilted.

SHRIMP WITH LOBSTER SAUCE

PREPARATION TIME: 15 MINUTES   CANTON
MARINATING TIME: 30 MINUTES
COOKING TIME: 8 MINUTES

1   pound (about 32–35) medium shrimp, shelled and
    deveined

MARINADE:
1   tablespoon cornstarch
1   tablespoon dry sherry

    2   tablespoons peanut oil

    1   tablespoon peanut oil

SEASONINGS:
2   teaspoons fermented black beans, soaked and minced
1   teaspoon minced garlic
2   whole scallions, minced

    ¼   cup lean, ground pork

SAUCE:
1   tablespoon soy sauce
1   tablespoon dry sherry
½   cup water
½   teaspoon salt
½   teaspoon sugar

    1   egg, lightly beaten

TO PREPARE:
    Combine ingredients for marinade and mix until smooth.
Add shrimp and set aside for 30 minutes.

ON THE TRAY:
    Bottle of peanut oil
    Bowl containing marinated shrimp
    Cup containing seasonings
    Cup containing pork

Bowl containing sauce
Cup containing egg

TO COOK:

To a heated wok add 2 tablespoons peanut oil. When oil is
hot add marinated shrimp and stir-fry 1 minute until shrimp turn
pink. Remove shrimp from wok and set aside in a bowl.

In the same wok heat 1 tablespoon peanut oil. Add seasonings and stir-fry 30 seconds. Add pork and stir-fry about 2 minutes
until it loses its pink color. Add sauce and stir until it comes to a
boil. Add shrimp and stir about 1 minute until heated through.
Add beaten egg. (There should be delicate shreds of egg running
through the sauce.) Remove from heat and serve immediately.

STIR-FRIED SPINACH

PREPARATION TIME: 10 MINUTES   CANTON
COOKING TIME: 3 MINUTES

1 *pound fresh spinach, washed and drained (tear apart
   larger leaves)*
3 *tablespoons peanut oil*
½ *teaspoon minced garlic*
½ *teaspoon salt*
½ *teaspoon sugar*

TO COOK:

To a heated wok add peanut oil. When oil is hot add salt,
then garlic, and stir-fry 30 seconds. Add spinach, then sugar, and
stir-fry about 2 minutes, until spinach is wilted. Remove from
heat and serve immediately.

MENU 9

SERVES TWO

Cherry Blossom Pork
Spicy Baby Shrimp
Boiled Rice

Cherry Blossom Pork is a variation of a sweet and sour dish using maraschino cherries for the sweet taste. A favorite at the Mandarin Inn, it can be prepared ahead and reheated.

The shrimp dish is mildly spicy. Remember you can vary the spiciness by adding more or less chili paste.

CHERRY BLOSSOM PORK

PREPARATION TIME: 20 MINUTES   PEKING
MARINATING TIME: 30 MINUTES
COOKING TIME: 15 MINUTES

1   *pound lean, boneless pork, thinly sliced into*
    ¼ × 1 × 1-inch slices

MARINADE:
1   *egg*
4   *tablespoons cornstarch*
½   *teaspoon salt*

4   *cups peanut oil for deep frying*

2   *tablespoons peanut oil*

½   *teaspoon minced fresh ginger*

VEGETABLES:
½   *cup fresh or frozen snow peas, stems and strings removed,*
    and cut in half
½   *cup sliced fresh or canned mushrooms*
15 *maraschino cherries, syrup washed off*

SAUCE:
¾   *cup canned chicken broth*
2   *tablespoons soy sauce*
⅓   *cup sugar*
⅓   *cup white rice vinegar*
¼   *teaspoon white pepper*

1   *tablespoon cornstarch, dissolved in 2 tablespoons*
    cold water

TO PREPARE:
    Combine ingredients for marinade and mix until smooth.
Add pork slices and set aside for 30 minutes.

ON THE TRAY:
    Bottle of peanut oil
    Bowl containing marinated pork

Cup containing ginger
Bowl containing vegetables
Bowl containing sauce
Cup containing dissolved cornstarch

TO COOK:
Step 1:
Heat 4 cups of peanut oil to 375° in a deep-fat fryer. Deep fry pork slices about 3 minutes until golden brown. Drain on paper towels and keep warm in a low, 200° oven until ready to combine with sauce. Reserve peanut oil in a covered jar to be used another time.

Step 2:
To a heated wok add 2 tablespoons peanut oil. When oil is hot add ginger and stir. Add vegetables and stir-fry 1 minute. Add sauce and stir until it comes to a boil. Add cornstarch and stir until thickened, about 1 minute. Add cooked pork to the sauce. Remove from heat and serve immediately.

SPICY BABY SHRIMP

PREPARATION TIME: 20 MINUTES   SZECHUAN
MARINATING TIME: 30 MINUTES
COOKING TIME: 5 MINUTES

½ *pound (about 50) baby shrimp, shelled and deveined*

MARINADE:
1   *tablespoon dry sherry*
1   *tablespoon cornstarch*
¼   *teaspoon salt*

2   *tablespoons peanut oil*

1   *tablespoon peanut oil*

SEASONINGS:
½   *teaspoon minced garlic*
½   *teaspoon minced fresh ginger*
1   *whole scallion, minced*

VEGETABLES:

½ cup diced canned bamboo shoots
½ cup frozen peas, thawed

SAUCE:

2 tablespoons dry sherry
3 tablespoons catsup
3 tablespoons water
1 teaspoon sugar
½ teaspoon salt
½ teaspoon chili paste with garlic

1 teaspoon sesame oil (optional)

TO PREPARE:

Combine ingredients for marinade and mix until smooth. Add shrimp and set aside 30 minutes.

ON THE TRAY:

Bottle of peanut oil
Bowl containing shrimp in marinade
Cup containing seasonings
Bowl containing vegetables
Bowl containing sauce
Bottle of sesame oil

TO COOK:

To a heated wok add 2 tablespoons peanut oil. When oil is hot add marinated shrimp and stir-fry 1 minute until they turn pink. Remove shrimp from wok and set aside in a bowl.

In the same wok heat 1 tablespoon peanut oil. Add seasonings and stir-fry 30 seconds. Add vegetables and stir-fry 1 minute. Add sauce and stir until it comes to a boil. Return shrimp to the wok and stir about 1 minute until heated through. Remove from heat and stir in sesame oil, if desired. Serve immediately.

MENU 10

SERVES TWO

Lamb with Scallions
Confucius Chicken
Boiled Rice

Although lamb is not commonly thought of as a Chinese meat, it is used extensively in the northern and Mongolian regions of the country. Lamb with Scallions is a stir-fried dish using shredded lamb. Remember, it is easier to shred the lamb if it is first slightly frozen.

Confucius Chicken is a dish of crisp, deep-fried pieces of chicken on a bed of watercress covered with a sauce of vegetables and crabmeat. The chicken can be fried and then kept warm in a low oven until it is combined with the sauce immediately before serving.

151

LAMB WITH SCALLIONS

MARINATING TIME: 30 MINUTES
COOKING TIME: 5 MINUTES

½ pound lean, boneless lamb, shredded

MARINADE:
2   *tablespoons dry sherry*
1   *tablespoon soy sauce*
1   *tablespoon cornstarch*

2   *tablespoons peanut oil*

2   *tablespoons peanut oil*

1   *teaspoon minced garlic*

4   *cups whole scallions, cut into 2-inch pieces*

½   *teaspoon salt*

1   *teaspoon sugar*

TO PREPARE:
Combine ingredients for marinade and mix until smooth.
Add shredded lamb and set aside 30 minutes.

ON THE TRAY:
Bottle of peanut oil
Cup containing garlic
Bowl containing marinated lamb
Bowl containing scallions
Salt
Sugar

TO COOK:
To a heated wok add 2 tablespoons peanut oil. When oil is
hot add garlic and stir-fry 30 seconds. Add marinated lamb and
stir-fry about 2 minutes until meat loses its pink color. Remove
lamb and set aside in a bowl.

In the same wok heat 2 tablespoons peanut oil and add the scallions. Stir-fry about 1 minute until the scallions are wilted. Add salt and sugar and stir. Return lamb to the wok and stir about 1 minute until heated through. Remove from heat and serve immediately.

CONFUCIUS CHICKEN

PREPARATION TIME: 30 MINUTES   PEKING
COOKING TIME: 8 MINUTES

- 2 *whole chicken breasts, skinned and boned*
- 1 *egg, lightly beaten*
- ½ *cup cornstarch*
- 4 *cups peanut oil for deep frying*
- 1 *bunch watercress*
- 2 *tablespoons peanut oil*
- ½ *teaspoon minced fresh ginger*

SAUCE:
- 3 *tablespoons soy sauce*
- 3 *tablespoons dry sherry*
- 1 *cup canned chicken broth*
- 1 *teaspoon sugar*
- ½ *teaspoon salt*

- ¼ *cup fresh or frozen crabmeat, broken into small pieces and picked through to remove cartilage*
- ¼ *cup sliced fresh or canned mushrooms*
- ½ *cup fresh or frozen snow peas, stems and strings removed, and cut in half*

- 1 *tablespoon cornstarch, dissolved in 2 tablespoons cold water*

TO PREPARE:
Cut each chicken breast into 4 large pieces. Dip in egg, then in cornstarch, and set aside on a plate to deep fry.

Trim tough stems of watercress and discard. Bring 1 quart of water to a boil. Add watercress, stir, then drain.

ON THE TRAY:

Bottle of peanut oil
Platter containing chicken pieces
Cup containing ginger
Bowl containing sauce
Bowl containing crabmeat, mushrooms, and peas
Cup containing dissolved cornstarch

TO COOK:

Step 1:

Heat 4 cups of peanut oil to 350° in a deep-fat fryer. Deep fry chicken pieces about 3 minutes until golden brown. Drain on paper towels and keep warm in a low, 200° oven until ready to combine with the sauce. Reserve cooking oil in a covered jar to be used again.

Step 2:

To a heated wok add 2 tablespoons peanut oil. When oil is hot add ginger and stir-fry 30 seconds. Add sauce and when it comes to a boil add crabmeat, mushrooms, and peas. Stir about 1 minute until heated through. Add cornstarch and stir about 1 minute until thickened. Remove from heat.

TO SERVE:

Arrange blanched watercress on a platter. Cut each piece of chicken into ½-inch slices and place on watercress. Pour the crabmeat and vegetable sauce over the chicken. Serve immediately.

MENU 11

SERVES FOUR

Mandarin Soup
Lemon Chicken
Ants Climbing a Tree
Sweet and Sour Carrots
Boiled Rice

We move on now to menus for four people. In this dinner the chicken requires marinating for at least 6 hours, so be sure to allow enough time in your schedule. The Ants Climbing a Tree gets its unusual name from its appearance. The bits of ground beef mixed with the noodles are supposed to suggest ants in the branches of a tree, but we hope this image won't prevent you from trying this tasty dish. It is quite hot so use less chili paste if

155

you prefer it milder. "Ants" can be made ahead and reheated in
the oven at 350° for 30 minutes. Mandarin Soup is a variation
of Egg Drop Soup. Sweet and Sour Carrots round out the meal.

MANDARIN SOUP

PREPARATION TIME: 15 MINUTES   PEKING
COOKING TIME: 8–10 MINUTES

    4   cups canned chicken broth
    2   tablespoons soy sauce
    1   tablespoon dry sherry
    ½   cup lean, boneless pork, shredded
    3   tablespoons cornstarch, dissolved in 3 tablespoons
        cold water
    2   eggs, lightly beaten
    1   teaspoon sesame oil
    1   whole scallion, thinly sliced

TO COOK:
Bring chicken broth to a boil. Add soy sauce, sherry, and
pork. Bring to a boil again, cover, and lower heat. Simmer 5
minutes. Add dissolved cornstarch and stir about 1 minute until
thickened. Add eggs slowly, stirring constantly. Remove from
heat and stir in sesame oil. Garnish with scallion and serve
immediately.

LEMON CHICKEN

PREPARATION TIME: 20 MINUTES   PEKING
MARINATING TIME: 6 HOURS OR OVERNIGHT
COOKING TIME: 3 MINUTES

    2   whole chicken breasts, skinned, boned, and shredded

MARINADE:

2 egg whites
2 tablespoons dry sherry
½ teaspoon salt
¼ teaspoon white pepper
¼ cup cornstarch, dissolved in ¼ cup cold water
2 tablespoons chopped fresh coriander or parsley
2 tablespoons peanut oil

   4 cups peanut oil for deep frying

   ½ head iceberg lettuce, shredded

   1 fresh lemon

TO PREPARE:

Combine ingredients for marinade and mix until smooth. Add chicken and mix with your hands for 10 minutes. Place bowl containing chicken and marinade in the refrigerator uncovered for at least 6 hours or preferably overnight.

TO COOK:

Heat 4 cups of peanut oil to 350° in a deep-fat fryer. Add chicken continuously, a few pieces at a time to separate the shreds. Fry 1 minute. Drain on paper towels. Reserve cooking oil in a covered jar to be reused.

TO SERVE:

Arrange shredded lettuce on a platter. Place chicken on top and squeeze juice of lemon over the chicken. Serve immediately.

ANTS CLIMBING A TREE

PREPARATION TIME: 30 MINUTES   SZECHUAN
COOKING TIME: 6 MINUTES

   2 ounces cellophane noodles

   4 tablespoons peanut oil

SEASONINGS:

3   *whole scallions, chopped*
1   *tablespoon minced fresh ginger*

    ½ *pound lean, ground beef*

SAUCE:

1   *tablespoon dry sherry*
1   *tablespoon soy sauce*
2   *teaspoons chili paste with garlic*
1   *teaspoon salt*
½ *cup canned chicken broth*

TO PREPARE:

Place cellophane noodles in hot water for 30 minutes to soften. Drain well.

Chop through noodles with a cleaver or knife a few times so the pieces will not be too long.

ON THE TRAY:

    Bottle of peanut oil
    Cup containing seasonings
    Bowl containing ground beef
    Bowl containing sauce
    Bowl containing softened noodles

TO COOK:

To a heated wok add 4 tablespoons peanut oil. When oil is hot add seasonings and stir-fry 30 seconds. Add beef and stir-fry about 1 minute until it loses its pink color. Add sauce and stir. Reduce heat to medium and add noodles. Cook about 3 minutes until liquid cooks down. Remove from heat and serve immediately.

SWEET AND SOUR CARROTS

PREPARATION TIME: 10 MINUTES   CANTON
COOKING TIME: 4 MINUTES

    1   *pound carrots, thinly sliced at an angle*

SAUCE:

3 *tablespoons sugar*
1 *tablespoon white rice vinegar*
½ *cup water*
½ *teaspoon salt*

> 1 *tablespoon cornstarch, dissolved in 1 tablespoon*
>   *cold water*

TO PREPARE:

Bring 2 quarts of water to a boil, add carrots, and cook for 2 minutes. Drain and rinse in cold water.

TO COOK:

Combine ingredients for the sauce in a wok and bring to a boil. Add carrots. When sauce comes to a boil again, add dissolved cornstarch and stir about 1 minute until sauce is thickened. Remove from heat and serve immediately.

MENU 12

SERVES FOUR

Shrimp Balls
Spicy Hot Pepper Beef
Chicken with Walnuts
Bean Sprout Salad
Boiled Rice

Shrimp Balls are deep fried and can be served as an appetizer or a first course. If you have a blender, the mixture can be made in it so it is very smooth. The Shrimp Balls can be made ahead and refrigerated or frozen. They can then be reheated in peanut oil at 375° for 5 minutes or in the oven at 375° for 10 minutes before serving.

The Hot Pepper Beef is very spicy, so you may want to

adjust the flavor to your own taste. It will be easier to shred the beef if it is slightly frozen.

A nice accompaniment to the spicy beef is the milder Chicken with Walnuts.

Try to use fresh bean sprouts in the salad. See the directions for growing your own bean sprouts on pages 47–48.

SHRIMP BALLS (*makes 24–30 balls*)

PREPARATION TIME: 30 MINUTES   SHANGHAI
COOKING TIME: 15 MINUTES

1   *pound shrimp, shelled, deveined, and finely minced to a paste*
8   *canned water chestnuts, minced*
1   *whole scallion, minced*
½   *teaspoon minced garlic*
½   *teaspoon salt*
1   *tablespoon dry sherry*

2   *egg whites, beaten until they hold soft peaks*

4   *cups peanut oil for deep frying*

TO PREPARE:

Combine first 6 ingredients. Gently fold in beaten egg whites. Form 1-inch balls, using about 1 teaspoon of shrimp mixture for each ball.

TO COOK:

Heat 4 cups peanut oil to 375° in a deep-fat fryer. Fry shrimp balls, 6 at a time, about 2–3 minutes until golden brown. Drain on paper towels. Reserve cooking oil in a covered jar to be reused. Serve with Hot Mustard and Duck Sauces.

SPICY HOT PEPPER BEEF

PREPARATION TIME: 20 MINUTES   SZECHUAN
MARINATING TIME: 30 MINUTES
COOKING TIME: 6 MINUTES

1   pound flank steak, thinly sliced across the grain,
    then shredded

MARINADE:
1   egg
2   tablespoons cornstarch
½   teaspoon salt

    ¼   cup peanut oil

SEASONINGS:
1   teaspoon minced fresh ginger
1   teaspoon minced garlic

VEGETABLES:
1   carrot, cut into 2-inch shreds
2   celery ribs, cut into 2-inch shreds

SAUCE:
1   tablespoon dry sherry
1   teaspoon sugar
1   tablespoon chili paste with garlic
1   tablespoon hoisin sauce
2   tablespoons soy sauce
2   tablespoons water

    1   whole scallion, cut into 2-inch shreds

    1   teaspoon sesame oil (optional)

TO PREPARE:
    Combine ingredients for marinade and mix until smooth.
Add shredded beef and set aside for 30 minutes.

ON THE TRAY:
    Bottle of peanut oil
    Bowl containing marinated beef

Cup containing seasonings
Bowl containing vegetables
Bowl containing sauce
Cup containing scallion
Bottle of sesame oil

TO COOK:

To a heated wok add ½ cup peanut oil. When oil is hot, add beef and stir-fry about 2 minutes until it loses its pink color. Remove beef with a slotted spoon and set aside in a bowl.

Pour off all but 2 tablespoons of oil. Add seasonings and stir-fry 30 seconds. Add vegetables and stir-fry 2 minutes. Add sauce and scallion and stir. Return beef to wok and heat thoroughly, about 1 minute. Remove from heat and stir in sesame oil, if desired. Serve immediately.

CHICKEN WITH WALNUTS

PREPARATION TIME: 30 MINUTES   CANTON
MARINATING TIME: 30 MINUTES
COOKING TIME: 10 MINUTES

2   *whole chicken breasts, skinned, boned, and cut into*
    1-inch cubes

MARINADE:
1   *egg*
2   *tablespoons cornstarch*
½   *teaspoon salt*
1   *teaspoon dry sherry*

    ½ *cup shelled walnut pieces*

    4 *cups peanut oil for deep frying*

    1 *tablespoon peanut oil*

    1 *teaspoon minced garlic*

VEGETABLES:

½ cup frozen peas, thawed
½ cup sliced canned or fresh mushrooms
6   canned water chestnuts, sliced

SAUCE:

1   tablespoon dry sherry
1   cup canned chicken broth
¼   teaspoon salt
1   teaspoon sugar

   1   tablespoon cornstarch, dissolved in 2 tablespoons
        cold water

TO PREPARE:

Combine ingredients for marinade and mix until smooth.
Add chicken cubes and set aside for 30 minutes. Place walnut
meats in a bowl and cover with boiling water. Let stand 5 minutes. Drain well. Peel off brown skin.

ON THE TRAY:

   Bottle of peanut oil
   Bowl containing blanched walnuts
   Bowl containing marinated chicken
   Cup containing garlic
   Bowl containing vegetables
   Bowl containing sauce
   Cup containing dissolved cornstarch

TO COOK:

Step 1:

Heat 4 cups peanut oil to 300° in a deep-fat fryer. Place
blanched walnuts in a sieve and deep fry about 30 seconds. Drain
on paper towels.

Increase heat of peanut oil to 375°. Deep fry chicken 2 minutes. Drain on paper towels. Reserve cooking oil in a covered jar
to reuse.

Step 2:

To a heated wok add 1 tablespoon peanut oil. When oil is

hot add garlic, and stir. Add vegetables and stir-fry 1 minute. Add sauce and stir about 1 minute until it boils. Add cornstarch and stir about 1 minute until it is thickened. Add chicken and walnuts and stir about 1 minute until heated through. Remove from heat and serve immediately.

BEAN SPROUT SALAD

PREPARATION TIME: 5 MINUTES   PEKING
CHILLING TIME: 1 HOUR

1   *pound fresh bean sprouts, or 1 can, drained*

DRESSING:
1   *teaspoon sugar*
1   *teaspoon white rice vinegar*
1   *tablespoon soy sauce*
1   *tablespoon sesame oil*

TO PREPARE:
Place fresh bean sprouts in a colander and pour over 2 quarts of boiling water to blanch them. Drain well and refrigerate. Combine ingredients for the dressing and refrigerate. Toss bean sprouts and dressing together just before serving.

MENU 13

SERVES FOUR

Paper-Wrapped Chicken
Shrimp with Sizzling Rice Soup
Rice Cakes
Szechuan Double-Cooked Pork
Mushrooms, Water Chestnuts, and Peas
Boiled Rice

Paper-Wrapped Chicken is unique. Boneless pieces of breast of chicken and spices are wrapped, envelope style, in waxed paper and deep fried. The paper holds in the juices and melds the flavors. The Chinese use rice paper but the more easily available waxed paper can also be used. (Do not use aluminum foil—the wrapper must be porous.)

166

The soup, too, is exceptional. Hot, crisp pieces of rice are added to the soup at the last minute, causing it to sizzle. The crispy rice pieces must be made two days ahead, so plan on it.

Szechuan Double-Cooked Pork, a spicy dish, gets its name because it is cooked twice. First it is boiled, and then it is stir-fried with the vegetables. It can be made ahead and reheated, but do not add cornstarch until just before serving.

The mushrooms, water chestnuts, and peas combine to make an interesting vegetable dish, which can be made ahead with the peas added just before serving.

PAPER-WRAPPED CHICKEN (*makes about 24 pieces*)

PREPARATION TIME: 20 MINUTES   PEKING
MARINATING TIME: 30 MINUTES
COOKING TIME: 12 MINUTES

1   *whole chicken breast, skinned, boned, and cut into*
     ¼ × 1 × 1½-inch slices

MARINADE:
1   *tablespoon soy sauce*
1   *tablespoon dry sherry*
½   *teaspoon minced fresh ginger*

2   *whole scallions, cut into 1-inch pieces and cut in half*
     lengthwise

24 *pieces waxed paper, cut into 4-inch squares*

4   *cups peanut oil for deep frying*

TO PREPARE:

Combine chicken with marinade and set aside 30 minutes. Rub peanut oil on waxed paper squares. Place 1 piece of chicken and 1 piece of scallion on 1 paper square. Turn up the bottom corner of the paper, covering the chicken and the scallion. Turn in the left corner and then the right corner of the paper, envelope style. Fold packet in half and tuck in the top flap. Continue until all of chicken and scallions are wrapped.

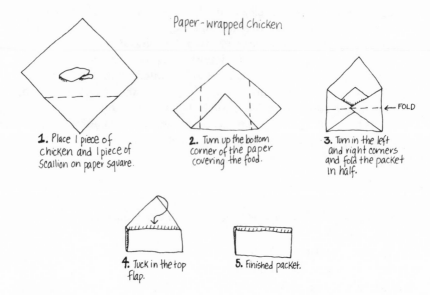

Paper-wrapped chicken

1. Place 1 piece of chicken and 1 piece of scallion on paper square.

2. Turn up the bottom corner of the paper covering the food.

3. Turn in the left and right corners and fold the packet in half.

← FOLD

4. Tuck in the top flap.

5. Finished packet.

TO COOK:

Heat 4 cups peanut oil to 350° in a deep-fat fryer. Fry chicken pieces 4 at a time. Turn after cooking 1 minute and cook the other side for 1 minute. Remove from oil and drain on paper towels. Reserve cooking oil in a covered jar to be reused.

TO SERVE:

Serve chicken pieces immediately, still wrapped in the paper. Guests will tear open the paper and eat the chicken and scallion with chopsticks.

SHRIMP WITH SIZZLING RICE SOUP

PREPARATION TIME: 30 MINUTES   SZECHUAN
(TWO DAYS REQUIRED FOR THE RICE CAKES, see following recipe)
COOKING TIME: 8 MINUTES

    4   *cups canned chicken broth*
   ½   *teaspoon salt*
   ¼   *teaspoon white pepper*

   ¼   *pound small shrimp, shelled and deveined*

VEGETABLES:

¼ cup carrots, diced in ½-inch pieces
¼ cup canned bamboo shoots, diced in ½-inch pieces
¼ cup canned water chestnuts, diced in ½-inch pieces
¼ cup frozen peas

    2   tablespoons cornstarch, dissolved in 2 tablespoons
        cold water

    2   teaspoons dry sherry

    4   cups peanut oil for deep frying

    2   cups rice cakes (see following recipe)

TO COOK:

Step 1:

Bring chicken broth to a boil with salt and pepper. Add shrimp and vegetables, cover, reduce heat, and simmer 3 minutes. Add dissolved cornstarch and stir until thickened, about 1 minute. Add sherry and stir. Remove from heat and pour into a large tureen.

Step 2:

Heat 4 cups of peanut oil to 375° in a deep-fat fryer. Fry pieces of rice about 2 minutes until golden brown. Drain on paper towels. Reserve cooking oil in a covered jar to be reused.

TO SERVE:

Bring the soup tureen and the plate of *hot* crisp rice pieces to the table separately. Combine rice and soup at the table to make a sizzling sound as the hot oil from the rice hits the broth.

RICE CAKES (*makes about 2 cups*)

PREPARATION TIME: 2 DAYS
COOKING TIME: 20 MINUTES

    1   cup rice
    2   cups cold water

TO COOK:

Step 1:

Combine water and rice in a 1-quart saucepan. Bring to a boil, cover, turn heat to low and simmer 20 minutes.

Step 2:

Let rice cool in the saucepan about 30 minutes. Press the rice down in a 9 × 13-inch baking pan, covering the bottom to make a thin layer. Set aside in a dry place (unused oven or countertop) for 2 days so that the rice dries out and becomes one crisp piece. Break rice into smaller pieces about 1 × 2 inches, and store in a plastic bag until ready to fry.

SZECHUAN DOUBLE-COOKED PORK

PREPARATION TIME: 20 MINUTES   SZECHUAN
COOKING TIME: 10 MINUTES

½ pound lean, boneless pork tenderloin, cut into
    ¼ × 1 × 1-inch slices

1 quart boiling water

3 tablespoons peanut oil

SEASONINGS:
1 tablespoon minced fresh ginger
1 tablespoon minced garlic

VEGETABLES:
¼ head round, green cabbage, cut into 1-inch pieces
1 green pepper, cut into 1-inch pieces
½ cup leeks, cut into 1-inch pieces

SAUCE:
3 tablespoons dry sherry
4 tablespoons soy sauce
2 tablespoons hoisin sauce
1 teaspoon sugar
1 tablespoon water
½ teaspoon chili paste with garlic

1   *tablespoon cornstarch, dissolved in 2 tablespoons*
    cold water

1   *teaspoon sesame oil (optional)*

ON THE TRAY:
Bowl containing pork slices
Bottle of peanut oil
Cup containing seasonings
Bowl containing vegetables
Cup containing sauce
Cup containing dissolved cornstarch
Bottle of sesame oil

TO COOK:
Step 1:
Bring 1 quart of water to a boil. Add pork slices and simmer 3 minutes. Drain on paper towels.

Step 2:
To a heated wok add 3 tablespoons peanut oil. When oil is hot add seasonings. Stir, then add the vegetables and stir-fry 2 minutes. Add the sauce and the pork and stir about 1 minute until it boils. Add cornstarch and stir until sauce is thickened, about 1 minute. Remove from heat and stir in sesame oil, if desired. Serve immediately.

MUSHROOMS, WATER CHESTNUTS, AND PEAS

PREPARATION TIME: 10 MINUTES   CANTON
COOKING TIME: 5 MINUTES

½   *pound fresh, whole mushroom caps*
1   *cup frozen peas, thawed*
8   *canned water chestnuts, sliced*
2   *tablespoons peanut oil*
½   *teaspoon salt*
1   *tablespoon oyster sauce*

TO COOK:

To a heated wok add 2 tablespoons peanut oil. When oil is hot add salt, then mushrooms. Reduce heat to medium and stir-fry 2 minutes. Add peas and water chestnuts and stir-fry 1 minute. Stir in oyster sauce. Remove from heat and serve immediately.

MENU 14

SERVES FOUR

Mu Shu Pork with Pancakes
Spicy Orange Chicken
Almond Fried Rice
Baby Corn with Snow Peas

Mu Shu Pork is a combination of exotic vegetables, eggs, and pork rolled in a thin pancake and eaten with the fingers. The pancakes are the same ones served with the Peking Duck. Both the filling and the pancakes can be made ahead and reheated separately.

Spicy Orange Chicken is a special recipe of Alex Wong, the chef at the Mandarin Inn restaurant. His use of both red and green peppers results in a colorful dish.

The Almond Fried Rice can be made ahead and reheated in the oven at 350° for 30 minutes. Remember the ingredients are optional, so let your imagination run wild. Always cook the rice the day before it is to be used in fried rice. The rice must be cold or it will stick together.

Baby ears of corn and snow peas are combined for the vegetable. Baby corn is available in cans, and the entire tiny ear is eaten.

MU SHU PORK

PREPARATION TIME: 30 MINUTES   PEKING
MARINATING TIME: 30 MINUTES
COOKING TIME: 7 MINUTES

½ pound lean, boneless pork, shredded

MARINADE:
1 tablespoon soy sauce
1 teaspoon cornstarch
1 teaspoon sugar
1 tablespoon dry sherry
½ teaspoon salt

2 tablespoons peanut oil

VEGETABLES:
½ cup dried tiger lily buds, soaked in warm water for 30 minutes
¼ cup dried tree ears, soaked in warm water for 30 minutes
*6 dried Chinese mushrooms, soaked in warm water for
   30 minutes*
6 whole scallions, cut into 2-inch pieces and shredded
1 cup shredded iceberg lettuce

4 eggs, scrambled in 2 tablespoons peanut oil

½ teaspoon salt

1 teaspoon sesame oil (optional)

Mandarin pancakes (see pages 124–25)

TO PREPARE:

Combine ingredients for marinade and mix until smooth. Add pork to marinade and set aside 30 minutes.

Remove and discard hard stem ends of the tiger lilies. Rinse well and pull in half lengthwise. Rinse the tree ears well to remove any sand, and shred. Rinse mushrooms, discard tough stems, and shred.

ON THE TRAY:

Bottle of peanut oil
Bowl containing marinated pork
Bowl containing vegetables
Cup containing scrambled eggs
Salt
Bottle of sesame oil

TO COOK:

To a heated wok add 2 tablespoons peanut oil. When oil is hot, add pork and stir-fry 3 minutes until it loses its pink color. Add vegetables and stir-fry 2 minutes. Add eggs and salt and stir-fry 1 minute. Remove from heat and stir in sesame oil, if desired. Serve with Mandarin Pancakes.

TO SERVE:

Place bowl of Mu Shu Pork on the table along with a platter of Mandarin Pancakes. Each guest spreads a pancake on his plate, places a heaping tablespoon of filling in the center of the pancake, and rolls it around the filling like a cigar. It is eaten with the fingers.

SPICY ORANGE CHICKEN

PREPARATION TIME: 1 HOUR   SZECHUAN
MARINATING TIME: 30 MINUTES
COOKING TIME: 6 MINUTES

2   whole chicken breasts, skinned, boned, and cut into
    ½-inch cubes

MARINADE:
1   egg
3   tablespoons cornstarch
½   teaspoon salt
1   tablespoon peanut oil

   ¼   cup peanut oil

   2   tablespoons peanut oil

   Peel from 1 orange, the white part discarded

SEASONINGS:
½   teaspoon minced garlic
1   tablespoon minced fresh ginger

VEGETABLES:
½   green pepper, cut into ½-inch cubes
½   red pepper, cut into ½-inch cubes

SAUCE:
½   teaspoon chili paste with garlic
4   tablespoons soy sauce
4   tablespoons dry sherry
4   tablespoons water
2   tablespoons sugar

   1   teaspoon cornstarch, dissolved in 2 teaspoons cold water

   1   teaspoon sesame oil (optional)

TO PREPARE:
   Combine ingredients for marinade and mix until smooth. Add chicken and set aside 30 minutes.
   Set orange peel aside to dry at least 1 hour. Then break into small 1-inch pieces.

ON THE TRAY:
   Bottle of peanut oil
   Bowl containing marinated chicken
   Cup containing orange peel
   Cup containing seasonings
   Cup containing vegetables

Cup containing sauce
Cup containing dissolved cornstarch
Bottle of sesame oil

TO COOK:

To a heated wok add ¼ cup peanut oil. When oil is hot, add chicken and stir-fry about 2 minutes until it loses its pink color. Remove chicken from wok and set aside in a bowl.

In the same wok heat 2 tablespoons peanut oil. Add orange peel and stir-fry about 30 seconds until it turns black. Add seasonings and stir. Add vegetables and stir-fry 1 minute. Add sauce and stir until it comes to a boil. Return chicken to wok and stir 1 minute until it is heated through. Add cornstarch and stir until thickened, about 1 minute. Remove from heat and stir in sesame oil, if desired. Serve immediately.

ALMOND FRIED RICE

PREPARATION TIME: 15 MINUTES   CANTON
COOKING TIME: 6 MINUTES

4   cups cold cooked rice. See pages 65–66.

4   tablespoons peanut oil

½   cup chopped whole scallions

2   eggs, scrambled in 2 tablespoons oil

½   cup slivered canned toasted almonds

SAUCE:
2   tablespoons soy sauce
½   teaspoon salt
½   teaspoon sugar

ON THE TRAY:
Bottle of peanut oil
Bowl containing scallions

Bowl containing cold cooked rice
Cup containing eggs
Cup containing almonds
Cup containing sauce

TO COOK:

To a heated wok add 4 tablespoons peanut oil. When oil is
hot add scallions and stir-fry 1 minute. Add cooked rice and stir-
fry about 3 minutes until it is heated through. Stir in eggs and
almonds. Add sauce and stir to blend. Heat about 1 minute.
Remove from heat and serve immediately.

BABY CORN WITH SNOW PEAS

PREPARATION TIME: 10 MINUTES   CANTON
COOKING TIME: 5 MINUTES

1   *can baby ears of corn, drained and sliced in half
    lengthwise (save liquid)*

½   *pound fresh or frozen snow peas, stems and strings
    removed*

2   *tablespoons peanut oil*

½   *teaspoon minced garlic*

SAUCE:
1   *teaspoon soy sauce*
2   *tablespoons dry sherry*
1   *teaspoon sugar*
½   *cup reserved liquid from corn*
½   *teaspoon salt*

1   *teaspoon cornstarch, dissolved in 2 teaspoons cold water*

ON THE TRAY:
Bottle of peanut oil
Cup containing garlic
Bowl containing snow peas
Bowl containing corn ears

Cup containing sauce
Cup containing dissolved cornstarch

TO COOK:

To a heated wok add 2 tablespoons peanut oil. When oil is hot add garlic. Stir, then add snow peas and stir-fry 2 minutes. Add corn ears and stir. Add sauce and stir about 1 minute until it boils. Add dissolved cornstarch and stir until it is thickened, about 1 minute. Remove from heat and serve immediately.

MENU 15

SERVES SIX

Fried Won Tons with Sweet and Sour Sauce
Dragon Soup
Beef with Broccoli
Soy Chicken
Steamed Chinese Sausage
Scallop Delight
Boiled Rice

Won tons are delicious when deep fried. They can be made ahead and frozen (see recipe for Won Tons), then deep fried just before serving. They are good served with Hot Mustard and Duck Sauces (see recipes), or with this Sweet and Sour Sauce.

Dragon Soup is a combination of chicken, crabmeat, and snow peas in broth. Deep-fried cellophane noodles can be added as a garnish just before serving, but they are optional. The soup tastes delicious without them as well.

Beef with Broccoli is a stir-fried dish and must be done at the last minute to maintain the crispness of the broccoli. It is one of the most popular Chinese dishes.

Soy Chicken, also called red-cooked chicken, is prepared ahead of time and can be served hot or at room temperature. The chicken is cooked in a "master sauce" that can be served with the chicken or saved, in the freezer, to be used again to prepare this recipe.

Chinese sausage is made from pork and has a sweet taste. It is sold in pairs tied together. In this menu it is very simply prepared. It is steamed and then sliced and served.

Scallop Delight is another dish from Alex Wong, the chef at the Mandarin Inn. He prefers to cook the sauce very slowly. We suggest you prepare the sauce at least 1 hour ahead and stir-fry the scallops just before serving. Incidentally, it is equally good served over shrimp.

FRIED WON TONS WITH SWEET AND SOUR SAUCE

PREPARATION TIME: 5 MINUTES   CANTON
COOKING TIME: 10 MINUTES

24 won tons, uncooked (see pages 95–97)

4 cups peanut oil for deep frying

1 cup canned chicken broth

½ cup sugar

½ cup white rice vinegar

1 tablespoon soy sauce

1 small can crushed pineapple with juice

1 tablespoon cornstarch, dissolved in 2 tablespoons cold water

TO COOK:

Step 1:

Heat 4 cups peanut oil to 350° in a deep-fat fryer. Add won

tons and fry about 6 minutes until golden brown. Drain on paper towels. Keep warm in a low, 200° oven while you are making the sauce. Reserve cooking oil in a covered jar to be used again.

Step 2:

Bring chicken broth to a boil. Add sugar, vinegar, soy sauce, and crushed pineapple. Stir until sugar is dissolved and it comes to a boil again. Add cornstarch and stir about 1 minute until the sauce is thickened.

TO SERVE:

Place fried won tons in a serving bowl and pour the sauce over them.

DRAGON SOUP

PREPARATION TIME: 10 MINUTES   PEKING
COOKING TIME: 10 MINUTES

6   *cups canned chicken broth*
½   *teaspoon salt*
¼   *teaspoon white pepper*

½   *cup diced boneless chicken*

½   *cup diced canned, fresh, or frozen crabmeat*

¼   *cup frozen peas, thawed*

3   *tablespoons cornstarch, dissolved in 3 tablespoons cold water*

1   *egg white, beaten with 2 tablespoons water until frothy*

2   *teaspoons dry sherry*

4   *cups peanut oil for deep frying*

½   *ounce cellophane noodles, cut into 2-inch lengths*

TO COOK:
Step 1:

Combine chicken broth, salt, and pepper and bring to a boil.

Add chicken, cover, and simmer 3 minutes. Remove cover and add crabmeat and peas. Add dissolved cornstarch and stir about 1 minute until thickened. Add egg white, stirring constantly. Add sherry and remove from heat.

Step 2:

Heat 4 cups peanut oil to 400° in a deep-fat fryer. Separate noodles and add to oil. Noodles will instantly puff up. Using tongs, turn noodles over and fry the other side. Remove from oil and drain on paper towels. Reserve cooking oil in a covered jar to be reused.

TO SERVE:

Place soup in a large tureen. Float fried cellophane noodles on top. Serve immediately.

BEEF WITH BROCCOLI

PREPARATION TIME: 20 MINUTES   CANTON
MARINATING TIME: 30 MINUTES
COOKING TIME: 7 MINUTES

   1   *pound flank steak, thinly sliced across the grain,*
        ¼ inch thick × 2 inches long

MARINADE:
1 *egg*
1 *teaspoon dry sherry*
¼ *teaspoon salt*
1 *tablespoon peanut oil*

   2 *tablespoons peanut oil*

   2 *tablespoons peanut oil*

   2 *cups sliced broccoli flowers*

SAUCE:
⅔ *cup canned chicken broth*
3 *tablespoons soy sauce*
1 *teaspoon sugar*
1 *tablespoon sherry*

   1   *tablespoon cornstarch, dissolved in 2 tablespoons*
       cold water

TO PREPARE:

   Combine ingredients for marinade and mix until smooth.
Add beef and set aside 30 minutes.

ON THE TRAY:

   Bottle of peanut oil
   Bowl containing marinated beef
   Bowl containing broccoli
   Bowl containing sauce
   Cup containing dissolved cornstarch

TO COOK:

   To a heated wok add 2 tablespoons peanut oil. When the oil
is hot add beef and stir-fry 2 minutes until it loses its pink color.
Remove beef from wok and set aside.

   In the same wok heat 2 tablespoons oil, add broccoli, and stir-
fry 1 minute. Add sauce, stir, and cover. Reduce heat and simmer
1 minute. Remove cover, return beef to wok, and stir until heated
through. Add cornstarch and stir about 1 minute until thickened.
Remove from heat and serve immediately.

SOY CHICKEN

PREPARATION TIME: 5 MINUTES   SHANGHAI
COOKING TIME: 1½ HOURS

   1   *4-pound whole chicken*

COOKING LIQUID:
1   *cup soy sauce*
2   *cups cold water*
¼   *cup dry sherry*
¼   *cup sugar*
3   *slices fresh ginger, about 1 inch in diameter* × ⅛ *inch thick*

Sesame oil

TO COOK:

Select a covered pot that will fit the chicken snugly and combine all the cooking ingredients, except the sesame oil, in the pot and bring to a boil. Add the chicken, breast side down. Bring to a boil again, cover, and reduce heat to simmer. Simmer 30 minutes, then turn chicken over and simmer another 30 minutes (1 hour total cooking time). Remove from the heat but keep pot covered and allow chicken to cool in the liquid for 30 minutes. Remove chicken from liquid and brush with sesame oil. If you do not plan to serve it within an hour, cover and refrigerate.

TO SERVE:

Chop chicken into bite-sized pieces, bones and all. Arrange on a platter, trying to reconstruct the shape of the chicken. Serve chilled or at room temperature, plain or with some of the cooking sauce.

STEAMED CHINESE SAUSAGE

PREPARATION TIME: 2 MINUTES   ALL REGIONS
COOKING TIME: 20 MINUTES

½ pound Chinese sausage (about 4 sausages)

Boiling water for steaming

Lettuce leaves

TO PREPARE:

Remove strings from the sausage and rinse in warm water.

TO COOK:

Bring water to a boil in a steamer. Place sausage on steamer rack lined with lettuce leaves. Cover and steam for 20 minutes. Remove sausage from steamer and slice diagonally into 1-inch pieces. Serve immediately.

SCALLOP DELIGHT

PREPARATION TIME: 20 MINUTES   PEKING
MARINATING TIME: 1 HOUR
COOKING TIME: 1 HOUR

> 1   *pound bay scallops, rinsed and drained*

MARINADE:
1   *egg*
2   *tablespoons cornstarch*
½   *teaspoon salt*

> *1 tablespoon peanut oil*

SEASONINGS:
1   *teaspoon minced garlic*
1   *teaspoon minced fresh ginger*
1   *whole scallion, minced*
½   *cup chopped onion*

SAUCE:
1   *cup canned chicken broth*
½   *cup canned crushed pineapple, including juice*
2   *tablespoons dry sherry*
3   *tablespoons catsup*
1   *teaspoon sugar*
½   *teaspoon salt*
1   *teaspoon white rice vinegar*
1   *teaspoon chili paste with garlic*

> *3 tablespoons peanut oil*

TO PREPARE:
Combine ingredients for marinade and mix until smooth. Add scallops and set aside in the refrigerator 1 hour while the sauce is cooking.

ON THE TRAY:
Bottle of peanut oil
Cup containing seasonings

Bowl containing sauce
Bowl containing marinated scallops

TO COOK:

Step 1:

To a heated wok add 1 tablespoon peanut oil. When oil is hot add seasonings and stir-fry 1 minute. Add sauce, cover, and reduce heat to simmer. Simmer 1 hour.

Step 2:

To a heated wok add 3 tablespoons peanut oil. When oil is hot add marinated scallops and stir-fry about 2 minutes. Remove scallops from wok and combine with sauce. Serve immediately.

MENU 16

SERVES SIX

Cold Drunken Chicken
Fried Butterfly Shrimp
Roasted Salt and Pepper
Ground Beef with Onions and Cellophane Noodles
Spicy Eggplant
Steamed Sea Bass in Brown Bean Sauce
Pork with Bean Sprouts
Boiled Rice

Cold Drunken Chicken is often served as part of the cold platter at banquets. Cut into bite-sized pieces and served with toothpicks it makes a fine cocktail appetizer.

Fried Butterfly Shrimp are dipped in a batter and deep fried. Leave the tail shell on so guests can hold it when they dip the shrimp in the Roasted Salt and Pepper. Instead of the Roasted Salt and Pepper, you can, if you prefer, use the Spicy Soy Dipping Sauce (see recipe).

Ground Beef with Onions and Cellophane Noodles is a stir-fried dish, so it is tastier if made at the last minute but it can be made ahead and reheated. The cellophane noodles can be fried a few hours ahead and heaped on top just before serving.

Spicy Eggplant is only mildly spicy. It can be made ahead and reheated.

The steamed fish calls for sea bass but you can substitute any white fish, such as flounder, snapper, etc. In selecting a fish to steam look for one that is firm and shiny with clear eyes. This will tell you the fish is fresh.

Pork with Bean Sprouts is another stir-fried dish and should be cooked at the last minute to preserve the crispness of the bean sprouts.

COLD DRUNKEN CHICKEN

PREPARATION TIME: 10 MINUTES   SHANGHAI
COOKING TIME: 20 MINUTES
MARINATING TIME: 24 HOURS

1   *whole chicken breast, skinned and boned*

2   *cups water*

SEASONINGS:
1   *whole scallion, cut into 2-inch pieces*
2   *slices fresh ginger, ⅛ inch thick × 1 inch in diameter*
½   *teaspoon salt*

½   *teaspoon salt*

½   *cup dry sherry*

TO COOK:
Step 1:

Bring water to a boil. Add seasonings and chicken breast.

Bring to a boil again, cover, and simmer 10 minutes. Turn off heat but do not remove cover from pot. Let stand for 10 minutes.

Step 2:

Remove chicken from broth and sprinkle with ½ teaspoon salt. Place chicken in a small bowl with the sherry, cover, and refrigerate overnight. Turn chicken occasionally while it is marinating.

TO SERVE:

Remove chicken from marinade, cut into 1-inch cubes, and serve cold.

FRIED BUTTERFLY SHRIMP

MARINATING TIME: 30 MINUTES   PEKING
COOKING TIME: 12 MINUTES

    1   *pound (about 24) large shrimp*

MARINADE:
1   *teaspoon dry sherry*
1   *teaspoon salt*

BATTER:
1   *cup all-purpose flour*
2   *teaspoons baking powder*
1   *cup water*

    4   *cups peanut oil for deep frying*

      Roasted salt and pepper for dipping

TO PREPARE:

Remove shell from shrimp, leaving the tail section intact. Make a cut along the back of the shrimp, splitting it about halfway through to butterfly the shrimp. Rinse under cold water to remove the black vein. Dry well on paper towels. Combine shrimp with marinade and set aside for 30 minutes. Combine ingredients for batter, mixing well until it is smooth.

TO COOK:

Heat 4 cups of peanut oil to 350° in a deep-fat fryer. Holding shrimp by the tail section, dip them, one at a time, into the batter. Fry the shrimp, 6 at a time, about 2 minutes until golden brown. Drain on paper towels and keep warm in a low, 200° oven until they are all fried. Serve with Roasted Salt and Pepper (see following recipe) or Spicy Soy Dipping Sauce. Reserve the cooking oil in a covered jar to be reused.

ROASTED SALT AND PEPPER

COOKING TIME: 5 MINUTES

3   tablespoons salt
1   teaspoon Szechuan peppercorns

TO COOK:

Place salt and peppercorns in a dry skillet over medium heat. Shake pan or stir the mixture while it cooks for about 5 minutes. Remove from the skillet and crush the mixture with a mortar and pestle or a rolling pin. Store in a covered jar.

GROUND BEEF WITH ONIONS AND CELLOPHANE NOODLES

PREPARATION TIME: 15 MINUTES   CANTON
MARINATING TIME: 30 MINUTES
COOKING TIME: 10 MINUTES

1   pound lean, ground round

MARINADE:
1   tablespoon soy sauce
1   tablespoon cornstarch
1   tablespoon dry sherry
1   teaspoon sugar

2   *tablespoons peanut oil*

2   *tablespoons peanut oil*

½   *teaspoon salt*

3   *cups thinly sliced onions*

¼   *teaspoon cayenne pepper*

2   *tablespoons oyster sauce*

1   *ounce cellophane noodles, cut into 2-inch lengths*

4   *cups peanut oil for deep frying*

TO PREPARE:

Combine ingredients for marinade and mix until smooth. Add beef and set aside 30 minutes.

ON THE TRAY:

Bottle of peanut oil
Bowl containing marinated beef
Salt
Bowl containing onions
Cayenne pepper
Bottle of oyster sauce
Cellophane noodles

TO COOK:

Step 1:

To a heated wok add 2 tablespoons peanut oil. When oil is hot, add beef and stir-fry about 2 minutes until it loses its pink color. Remove beef and set aside in a bowl.

In the same wok heat 2 tablespoons peanut oil, add salt and onions, and stir-fry 2 minutes. Return beef to wok and add cayenne pepper and oyster sauce. Stir to heat through and combine ingredients. Remove from heat.

Step 2:

Separate noodles. Heat 4 cups peanut oil to 400° in a deep-fat fryer. Place about half the noodles in the hot oil. They will instantly puff up. Using tongs, turn noodles over to briefly fry the other side. Remove from oil and drain on paper towels. Fry remaining noodles the same way. Reserve cooking oil in a covered jar to be reused.

TO SERVE:

Arrange beef and onions on a platter. Heap the fried noodles on top of the beef. Serve immediately.

SPICY EGGPLANT

PREPARATION TIME: 30 MINUTES   SZECHUAN
COOKING TIME: 6 MINUTES

1   *large eggplant, peeled and cut into 3 × ½-inch fingers*

¼   *pound lean, ground pork*

1   *tablespoon peanut oil*

3   *tablespoons peanut oil*

SEASONINGS:
1   *tablespoon minced fresh ginger*
1   *teaspoon minced garlic*

  10   *pieces dried shrimp, soaked in warm water 30 minutes, then chopped*

SAUCE:
1   *cup canned chicken broth*
3   *tablespoons soy sauce*
2   *tablespoons dry sherry*
1   *teaspoon white rice vinegar*
1½ *teaspoons sugar*
½   *teaspoon salt*
1   *tablespoon chili paste with garlic*

  1   *tablespoon cornstarch, dissolved in 2 tablespoons cold water*

  1   *tablespoon sesame oil (optional)*

  3   *whole scallions, chopped*

ON THE TRAY:
>Bottle of peanut oil
>Cup containing pork
>Cup containing seasonings
>Bowl containing eggplant
>Cup containing shrimp
>Bowl containing sauce
>Cup containing dissolved cornstarch
>Sesame oil
>Cup containing scallions

TO COOK:

To a heated wok add 1 tablespoon peanut oil. When the oil is hot, add pork and stir-fry about 1 minute until pork loses its pink color. Remove pork from wok and set aside in a bowl.

In the same wok heat 3 tablespoons peanut oil, add seasonings and stir. Add eggplant and stir-fry 2 minutes. Add shrimp and sauce and stir until sauce boils. Return pork to wok and stir. Add cornstarch and stir until sauce is thickened, about 1 minute. Remove from heat and stir in sesame oil, if desired. Garnish with scallions and serve immediately.

STEAMED SEA BASS IN BROWN BEAN SAUCE

PREPARATION TIME: 10 MINUTES   PEKING
COOKING TIME: 20 MINUTES

>1   *2-pound whole, fresh sea bass or other white fish,*
>   *cleaned, scaled, and gills removed*

SAUCE:
3   *teaspoons ground brown bean sauce*
2   *teaspoons soy sauce*
½   *teaspoon sugar*
½   *teaspoon salt*
1   *teaspoon peanut oil*
2   *teaspoons minced fresh ginger*
1   *teaspoon minced garlic*

2   *whole scallions, cut into 1-inch pieces*

TO PREPARE:

Make 3 diagonal slashes about 2 inches long from the back-bone toward the tail along each side of the fish.

Combine ingredients for the sauce and mix well. Spread sauce over the fish, and place scallions decoratively on top.

TO COOK:

Bring water to a boil in a steamer. Place fish on a plate 1 inch smaller than the steamer. If the fish is too large to fit into the steamer, cut it in half. Cover and steam for 20 minues.

TO SERVE:

Serve the whole fish with the sauce poured over it on a platter. If the fish has been cut in half to fit in the steamer, place the two halves together and cover the cut with the scallion pieces.

PORK WITH BEAN SPROUTS

PREPARATION TIME: 20 MINUTES   CANTON
MARINATING TIME: 30 MINUTES
COOKING TIME: 7 MINUTES

½   *pound lean, boneless pork, shredded*

MARINADE:
1   *tablespoon cornstarch*
1   *tablespoon dry sherry*
1   *tablespoon soy sauce*

1   *tablespoon peanut oil*

2   *tablespoons peanut oil*

¼   *cup minced onions*

½   *pound fresh bean sprouts, or 1 can, drained*

SAUCE:
¼ cup canned chicken broth
1   tablespoon soy sauce
½ teaspoon sugar

TO PREPARE:

Combine ingredients for marinade and mix until smooth. Add pork and marinate for 30 minutes.

Bring 2 quarts of water to a boil and pour over the bean sprouts if you are using fresh ones. Drain well.

ON THE TRAY:
Bottle of peanut oil
Bowl containing marinated pork
Bowl containing onions
Bowl containing bean sprouts
Bowl containing sauce

TO COOK:

To a heated wok add 1 tablespoon peanut oil. When the oil is hot, add pork and stir-fry about 3 minutes until it loses its pink color. Remove pork and set aside in a bowl.

In the same wok heat 2 tablespoons of peanut oil. Add onions and stir-fry 30 seconds. Add bean sprouts, toss to coat with oil, and stir-fry 1 minute. Add the sauce and stir until it comes to a boil. Return pork to wok and stir about 1 minute until heated through. Remove from heat and serve immediately.

MENU 17

SERVES SIX

Scallion Pancakes
Watercress Soup
Lion's Head
Spicy Mandarin Noodles
Jow La Chicken
Agar-Agar Salad

The Scallion Pancakes and Watercress Soup are a delicious combination for the first course of your dinner.

Lion's Head is a casserole dish that can be made ahead and then reheated in the oven before serving. Its unusual name comes from its appearance. The ground pork is formed into large meatballs and covered with strips of cabbage suggesting a lion's head and mane.

The noodle dish is a tasty combination of meat and vegetables poured over the noodles. It can be made ahead and reheated.

Jow La Chicken is crisp pieces of fried boneless chicken covered with a spicy sauce. The sprigs of coriander add an interesting flavor. However, if fresh coriander is not available, use regular parsley.

When you make the salad do not add the dressing until just before serving so the soy sauce does not darken the lettuce. We think you will like the seaweed for the texture it adds. If you cannot get agar-agar, simply leave it out. The ham and lettuce alone make an interesting salad.

SCALLION PANCAKES (*makes 6 pancakes*)

PREPARATION TIME: 45 MINUTES   PEKING
COOKING TIME: 6 MINUTES

2   *cups all-purpose flour*
1   *teaspoon salt*
1   *cup boiling water*

Peanut oil

½ *cup chopped whole scallions*

TO PREPARE:

Place flour and salt in a large mixing bowl. Gradually pour in boiling water, stirring with a wooden spoon to mix. When cool enough to handle, knead with your hands about 10 minutes until the dough is elastic. Place dough in a bowl and cover with a damp dish towel for 30 minutes.

Roll the dough out to a rectangular shape approximately ¼ × 10 × 15 inches. Brush the top lightly with peanut oil. Sprinkle scallions over the entire surface of the dough. Starting from one end, roll up the dough as you would a carpet. Cut the roll into 6 thick slices. Flatten each slice slightly with your hand. Roll out each piece, turning it to keep it circular, until it is ¼ inch thick and about 6 inches in diameter. Keep the finished pancakes covered with a damp towel while you are working.

TO COOK:

Heat skillet over high heat and pour in oil to ¼ inch deep. When oil is hot, turn heat to medium low. Cook pancakes one at a time, about 30 seconds on each side, until they are golden in color. Cut into wedges and serve warm.

Pancakes may be reheated in the oven before serving.

WATERCRESS SOUP

PREPARATION TIME: 10 MINUTES   PEKING
COOKING TIME: 5 MINUTES

1   *bunch watercress*
6   *cups canned chicken broth*
1   *teaspoon salt*
2   *tablespoons cornstarch, dissolved in 2 tablespoons*
    cold water
1   *teaspoon dry sherry*
1   *whole scallion, thinly sliced*

TO PREPARE:

Trim any tough stems from the watercress. Rinse in cold water, drain, and chop coarsely.

TO COOK:

Bring chicken broth and salt to a boil. Add watercress, cover, and lower heat. Simmer 2 minutes. Add cornstarch and stir about 1 minute until thickened. Stir in dry sherry. Remove from heat and garnish with scallion. Serve immediately.

LION'S HEAD

PREPARATION TIME: 20 MINUTES   YANGCHOW
COOKING TIME: 1 HOUR AND 10 MINUTES

MEATBALL MIXTURE:
1½ pounds lean, ground pork
8   canned water chestnuts, chopped
2   whole scallions, chopped
1   egg
¼   cup soy sauce
1   tablespoon dry sherry
½   teaspoon sugar
2   teaspoons cornstarch

2   tablespoons peanut oil

2   pounds celery cabbage, cut into ½-inch shreds

1   cup canned chicken broth

TO PREPARE:
   Combine meatball mixture and form 6 large meatballs. Mixture will be soft.

TO COOK:
   To a heated wok add 2 tablespoons peanut oil. When oil is hot brown the meatballs, one at a time, on all sides. Add more oil if necessary.
   Arrange half the sliced cabbage in the bottom of a flameproof casserole. Place the browned meatballs on the layer of cabbage. Place the remaining cabbage on top of the meatballs. Pour the chicken broth over this. Bring to a boil, cover, and lower heat. Simmer 1 hour, checking occasionally to be sure there is still liquid in the pot. If not, add a small amount of chicken broth. Remove from heat and serve immediately. This dish can be reheated.

SPICY MANDARIN NOODLES

PREPARATION TIME: 30 MINUTES   PEKING
COOKING TIME: 5 MINUTES

½ pound fresh Chinese egg noodles

2 tablespoons peanut oil

3 tablespoons peanut oil

¼ pound ground beef

VEGETABLES:
¼ cup diced red or green pepper
¼ cup diced canned bamboo shoots
6 dried Chinese mushrooms, soaked in warm water 30 minutes
2 cups bean sprouts

SAUCE:
1 tablespoon hoisin sauce
1 tablespoon ground brown bean sauce
2 tablespoons dry sherry
3 tablespoons soy sauce
1 teaspoon sugar
½ cup canned chicken broth
½ teaspoon chili paste with garlic

1 tablespoon cornstarch, dissolved in 2 tablespoons
cold water

1 whole scallion, thinly sliced

TO PREPARE:
Bring 6 quarts of water to a boil and cook noodles 2 minutes.
Drain and rinse with cold water. Mix with 2 tablespoons of peanut
oil.
Rinse mushrooms, discard tough stems, and dice.

ON THE TRAY:
Bottle of peanut oil
Bowl containing ground beef

Bowl containing vegetables
Bowl containing sauce
Cup containing dissolved cornstarch
Bowl containing noodles
Cup containing scallions

TO COOK:

To a heated wok add 3 tablespoons peanut oil. When oil is hot, add ground beef and stir-fry 1 minute, until it loses its pink color. Add vegetables and stir-fry 2 minutes. Add sauce and stir until blended. Add cornstarch and stir about 1 minute until thickened.

TO SERVE:

Pour boiling water over the noodles to reheat them. Drain. Place noodles on a serving platter and pour meat and vegetable sauce over them. Garnish with scallions and serve immediately.

JOW LA CHICKEN

PREPARATION TIME: 20 MINUTES   SZECHUAN
COOKING TIME: 10 MINUTES

2   whole chicken breasts, skinned, boned, and each breast
    cut into 4 large pieces
1   egg, lightly beaten
Cornstarch

4   cups peanut oil for deep frying

3   tablespoons peanut oil

4   dried red chili peppers, cut in half

SEASONINGS:
1   teaspoon minced fresh ginger
1   teaspoon minced garlic
2   whole scallions, minced

SAUCE:

3   tablespoons soy sauce
3   tablespoons white rice vinegar
3   tablespoons sugar
¾   cup canned chicken broth

    2   tablespoons cornstarch, dissolved in 2 tablespoons
       cold water

    6   sprigs fresh coriander or parsley

TO PREPARE:

    Dip chicken pieces into egg, then into cornstarch.

ON THE TRAY:

    Bottle of peanut oil
    Platter containing chicken pieces
    Cup containing dried red peppers
    Cup containing seasonings
    Cup containing sauce
    Cup containing dissolved cornstarch
    Sprigs of coriander

TO COOK:

Step 1:

    Heat 4 cups of peanut oil to 350° in a deep-fat fryer. Deep fry chicken 4 pieces at a time, about 3 minutes each until golden. Drain on paper towels. Reserve cooking oil in a covered jar to be reused.

Step 2:

    To a heated wok add 3 tablespoons peanut oil. When oil is hot, add dried red peppers and stir-fry about 30 seconds until they turn black. Add seasonings and stir. Add sauce and stir until it boils. Add cornstarch and stir about 1 minute until thckened. Remove from heat.

TO SERVE:

    Cut fried chicken into bite-sized pieces and arrange on a platter. Place coriander or parsley sprigs on top of chicken. Pour sauce from the wok over the chicken. Serve immediately.

AGAR-AGAR SALAD

½ *ounce dried agar-agar, cut into 2-inch strips*

½ *small head iceberg lettuce, shredded*

4 *slices boiled ham, cut into julienne strips*

DRESSING:

2 *tablespoons soy sauce*

2 *tablespoons sesame oil*

½ *teaspoon sugar*

1 *tablespoon white sesame seeds, toasted*

TO PREPARE:

Soak agar-agar in cold water for 15 minutes. Drain. Combine agar-agar, lettuce, and ham in a large salad bowl. Cover and refrigerate. Combine ingredients for dressing. Pour dressing over salad just before serving. Sprinkle with sesame seeds.

MENU 18

SERVES SIX

Pearl Balls
Winter Melon Soup
Spicy Clams
Buddha's Delight
Pepper Steak
Shanghai Duck
Steamed Bread

We begin this dinner with Pearl Balls, which are tasty meatballs lightly seasoned with fresh ginger, then rolled in glutinous rice and steamed. The translucent rice coating gives them their name.

If winter melon is not available for the soup, you may substitute cucumber. Their flavors are quite similar.

Spicy Clams are steamed open, then covered with a moderately spicy sauce. The sauce can be made ahead and reheated.

Buddha's Delight is a famous vegetarian dish that generally contains at least 10 different vegetables, both fresh and dried. However, you can eliminate some or add others if you wish. It can be cooked ahead and reheated before serving.

Pepper Steak is a stir-fried dish combining thinly sliced flank steak and green peppers. It should be cooked at the last minute to preserve the crispness of the peppers.

Shanghai Duck has been simmered first in spices, then roasted in the oven the next day. This process eliminates the greasiness often associated with roast duck. Steamed Bread is often served with duck rather than the Mandarin Pancakes. We give you a short-cut method for making steamed bread.

PEARL BALLS (*makes 3 dozen meatballs*)

PREPARATION TIME: 2 OR 3 HOURS   SZECHUAN
COOKING TIME: 30 MINUTES

1 *cup glutinous rice*

MEATBALL MIXTURE:
1 *pound lean, ground pork*
8 *dried Chinese mushrooms, soaked in warm water for 30 minutes*
8 *canned water chestnuts, finely chopped*
¼ *cup finely chopped canned bamboo shoots*
1 *teaspoon minced garlic*
2 *tablespoons minced fresh ginger*
2 *whole scallions, minced*
1 *egg*
1 *tablespoon soy sauce*
1½ *teaspoons salt*
½ *teaspoon sugar*

Lettuce leaves

TO PREPARE:

Rinse the rice and soak it in cold water for 2 or 3 hours.

Rinse mushrooms, discard tough stems, and chop fine. Combine meatball mixture thoroughly. With your hands form mixture into meatballs about 1 inch in diameter. Drain the rice and spread it out on a cloth towel. Roll the meatballs, one at a time, over the rice, pressing it in gently so the rice covers the meatball.

TO COOK:

Bring water to a boil in a steamer. Place meatballs on a steamer rack lined with lettuce leaves. Leave ½-inch space between them to allow for expansion as the rice cooks. Cover and steam for 30 minutes. Serve with Spicy Soy Dipping Sauce.

WINTER MELON SOUP

PREPARATION TIME: 30 MINUTES   CANTON
COOKING TIME: 20 MINUTES

6   cups canned chicken broth
½   teaspoon salt

1   pound winter melon

6   dried Chinese mushrooms, soaked in warm water
    30 minutes

¼   pound ham, diced

TO PREPARE:

Peel and remove the seeds from the melon and cut into slices 1 × 1 × ¼ inch thick. Rinse mushrooms, discard tough stems, and cut into quarters.

TO COOK:

Bring chicken broth and salt to a boil. Add melon slices, mushrooms, and ham. Bring to a boil again, cover, and turn to low heat. Simmer 15 minutes. Remove from heat and serve immediately.

SPICY CLAMS

PREPARATION TIME: 15 MINUTES   SZECHUAN
COOKING TIME: 15 MINUTES

36 hard-shell clams, littlenecks or cherrystones, washed
    and drained

2   tablespoons peanut oil

SEASONINGS:

1   teaspoon minced fresh ginger
1   teaspoon minced garlic

SAUCE:

2   cups canned chicken broth
¼   teaspoon salt
2   tablespoons soy sauce
1   teaspoon chili paste with garlic
3   tablespoons dry sherry
1   tablespoon oyster sauce

  2   tablespoons cornstarch, dissolved in 2 tablespoons
      cold water

  1   tablespoon sesame oil (optional)

  2   whole scallions, thinly sliced

ON THE TRAY:

Bottle of peanut oil
Cup containing seasonings
Bowl containing sauce
Cup containing dissolved cornstarch
Bottle of sesame oil
Bowl containing clams
Cup containing scallions

TO COOK:

Step 1:

To a heated wok add 2 tablespoons peanut oil. When oil is
hot add seasonings and stir. Add sauce and stir until it comes to

a boil. Add cornstarch and stir 1 minute until it is thickened. Remove from heat and stir in sesame oil, if desired.

Step 2:

Place clams in a large pot with cold water to cover. Cover pot and bring water to a boil. Boil 5–10 minutes or until the shells open. Drain.

TO SERVE:

Arrange cooked clams on a deep platter. Pour sauce over the clams. Garnish with scallions and serve immediately.

BUDDHA'S DELIGHT

PREPARATION TIME: 30 MINUTES   CANTON
COOKING TIME: 12 MINUTES

  1   cup sliced bok choy
  1   cup broccoli flowers
 16   dried tiger lily buds, soaked in warm water 30 minutes
 20   dried ginkgo nuts, shelled and soaked in boiling water
       15 minutes
  2   tablespoons tree ears, soaked in warm water 30 minutes
  4   dried lotus roots, soaked in hot water 30 minutes,
       drained, and sliced
 ¼   cup sliced canned water chestnuts
 ¼   cup sliced carrots
 ¼   cup canned baby ears of corn, drained and sliced in
       half lengthwise
 ¼   cup sliced canned bamboo shoots
 15   fresh or frozen snow peas, stems and strings removed

  3   tablespoons peanut oil

SAUCE:
  1   cup canned chicken broth
  1   tablespoon dry sherry
  1   teaspoon soy sauce
  1   teaspoon salt
 ½   teaspoon sugar

1   teaspoon cornstarch, dissolved in 2 teaspoons cold water

TO PREPARE:

Discard hard stem end of tiger lilies. Rinse tree ears to remove sand, and shred.

ON THE TRAY:

Bottle of peanut oil
Bowl containing bok choy
Bowl containing broccoli
Bowl containing remaining vegetables
Bowl containing sauce
Cup containing dissolved cornstarch

TO COOK:

To a heated wok add 3 tablespoons peanut oil. When the oil is hot add bok choy and stir-fry 1 minute. Add broccoli and stir-fry 1 minute. Add remaining vegetables and stir. Add sauce, cover, reduce heat, and simmer 10 minutes. Add cornstarch and simmer 1 minute until thickened. Remove from heat and serve immediately.

PEPPER STEAK

PREPARATION TIME: 15 MINUTES   CANTON
MARINATING TIME: 30 MINUTES
COOKING TIME: 5 MINUTES

1   pound flank steak, thinly sliced across the grain,
    ¼ inch thick × 2 inches long

MARINADE:

2   teaspoons cornstarch
3   tablespoons soy sauce
1   egg
1   teaspoon sugar

    3   tablespoons peanut oil

    2   tablespoons peanut oil

    2   green peppers, cut into 1-inch squares

TO PREPARE:

Combine ingredients for marinade and mix until smooth. Add beef and marinate 30 minutes.

ON THE TRAY:

Bottle of peanut oil
Bowl containing beef
Bowl containing green pepper

TO COOK:

To a heated wok add 3 tablespoons peanut oil. When oil is hot, add beef and stir-fry about 2 minutes until it loses its pink color. Remove beef from wok and set aside in a bowl.

In the same wok heat 2 tablespoons peanut oil. Add green pepper and stir-fry 2 minutes. Return beef to wok and stir to mix thoroughly. Remove from heat and serve immediately.

SHANGHAI DUCK

PREPARATION TIME: OVERNIGHT   SHANGHAI
COOKING TIME: 25 MINUTES

1   *4–5-pound duckling, thawed*

4   *slices fresh ginger, about 1 inch in diameter $\times$ ⅛ inch thick*

2   *whole scallions, cut into 2-inch pieces*

2   *teaspoons star anise*

¼   *cup dry sherry*
4   *tablespoons soy sauce*
2   *teaspoons sugar*
1   *cup water*

TO PREPARE:

Place duck, breast down, in a casserole that has been rubbed with oil. Place half the ginger and half the scallions in the cavity of the duck. Place the remainder of the ginger and scallions plus the star anise over the duck. Combine sherry, soy sauce, sugar, and water and pour over the duck. Turn heat to high and bring to a boil. Cover, turn heat to low; simmer 1½ hours, turning duck over on its back after 30 minutes. Remove casserole from heat, but let the duck stand in the liquid for 30 minutes. Remove duck from the liquid and place on an uncovered platter in the refrigerator overnight. Refrigerate the cooking liquid separately.

TO COOK:

Preheat oven to 500°. Place duck, breast down, on a rack in a roasting pan and cook for 15 minutes. Increase heat to 550°, turn duck breast up, and cook for 10 minutes.

TO SERVE:

Carve duck and skin in thin slices and arrange on a platter. Serve with Steamed Bread and Shanghai Sauce. (See following recipes.) Guests will make sandwiches with the duck and bread and spoon a little sauce over the top.

SHANGHAI SAUCE

Remove the cooking liquid (it has turned to jelly) from the refrigerator and discard the layer of fat that has formed on top. Bring the jelly to a boil and boil vigorously until it reduces to ½ cup. Strain and serve warm in a small bowl.

STEAMED BREAD

PREPARATION TIME: 10 MINUTES

COOKING TIME: 10 MINUTES

1 or 2 packages refrigerated biscuits

Sesame oil

Pieces of waxed paper cut into 3-inch squares

TO PREPARE:

Shape each biscuit into a 4-inch rectangle, making it slightly narrower in the center. Cover the surface of the biscuit with sesame oil. Fold the biscuit in half.

TO COOK:

Bring water to a boil in a steamer. Place each folded biscuit on a square of waxed paper and arrange in the steamer, leaving space between each biscuit for expansion as it steams. Steam for 10 minutes.

MORE RECIPES

SPRING ROLLS

PREPARATION TIME: 1 HOUR AND 45 MINUTES   SHANGHAI
COOKING TIME: 12 MINUTES

These are a variation of the egg roll, but the skins are lighter and more delicate, and they are more difficult to make. Use ready-made spring roll skins or the recipe below.

SPRING ROLL SKINS (*makes about 1 dozen*)
2   *cups all-purpose flour*
½   *teaspoon salt*
1½ *cups water*

TO PREPARE:
Combine flour and salt, then gradually add the water. Beat

the batter with a wire whisk or wooden spoon for about 15 minutes until it becomes smooth. Set aside for about 15 minutes.

TO COOK:

Lightly oil an 8-inch skillet or crêpe pan. Heat over a very low burner. Using a pastry brush, brush the batter over the entire surface of the skillet in a very thin layer. Let it set. Carefully remove the pancake from the skillet before it browns. Cover the finished skins with a dry towel. Lightly oil the skillet before making each one. Flour each skin so that they don't stick together, and wrap in foil. They may be refrigerated for 3 or 4 days or frozen until ready to fill.

SPRING ROLLS

FILLING:

½ cup lean, ground pork

½ cup chicken breast, skinned, boned, and shredded

2 cups medium shrimp, shelled, deveined, and cut into thirds

2 tablespoons peanut oil

3 tablespoons peanut oil

½ head large, round cabbage, finely shredded

8 dried Chinese mushrooms, soaked in warm water 30 minutes

3 whole scallions, chopped

SAUCE:

⅓ cup canned chicken broth
1½ teaspoons salt
3 tablespoons dry sherry
1 tablespoon sugar

2 teaspoons cornstarch, dissolved in 2 teaspoons cold water

1 tablespoon sesame oil

1 egg, lightly beaten

4 cups peanut oil for deep frying

12 spring roll skins (see preceding recipe)

TO PREPARE:

Rinse mushrooms, discard tough stems, and shred.

ON THE TRAY:

Bottle of peanut oil
Cup containing pork
Cup containing chicken
Bowl containing shrimp
Bowl containing cabbage
Cup containing mushrooms and scallions
Cup containing sauce
Cup containing dissolved cornstarch
Bottle of sesame oil
Cup containing egg

TO COOK:

To a heated wok add 2 tablespoons peanut oil. When the oil is hot, add pork and stir-fry 1 minute or until it loses its pink color. Add chicken and stir-fry 1 minute, until it loses its pink color. Add shrimp and stir-fry 1 minute or until they turn pink. Remove pork, shrimp, and chicken from the wok and set aside in a bowl.

In the same wok heat 3 tablespoons peanut oil. Add the cabbage and stir-fry about 2 minutes until it is wilted. Add mushrooms and scallions and stir. Add sauce and stir until it boils. Add cornstarch and stir about 1 minute until it is thickened. Return pork, chicken, and shrimp to the wok and stir. Stir in the sesame oil and set aside to cool before filling the skins.

TO ASSEMBLE: (*See illustration for Egg Rolls.*)

Cover the spring roll skins with a slightly dampened dish towel to prevent them from drying out while you are working. Carefully peel off one skin. Place on a lightly floured board. Using a slotted spoon (so the filling won't be too wet and split it) place about 2 tablespoons of filling below the center of the skin. Using a pastry brush, paint the outer edge with the beaten egg. Fold over the bottom edge to cover the filling. Fold in first the left side, then the right side of the skin. Now roll from the bottom until you have a cylinder. The beaten egg will hold it closed. Place sealed side down on a plate. Cover the spring rolls with a damp dish towel until ready to fry.

TO COOK:

Heat 4 cups peanut oil to 375° in a deep-fat fryer. Fry spring rolls 4 at a time, about 3 minutes until golden brown. Drain on paper towels. Reserve cooking oil in a covered jar to reuse. Cut spring rolls in thirds and serve with Hot Mustard and Duck Sauces.

FRIED DUMPLINGS (*makes about 3 dozen*)

PREPARATION TIME: 30 MINUTES   PEKING
COOKING TIME: 12 MINUTES

Round dumpling skins (see pages 108–09)

FILLING:
½ *pound lean, ground pork*
½ *cup finely chopped celery cabbage*
½ *cup finely chopped scallions*
½ *teaspoon minced fresh ginger*
1 *teaspoon dry sherry*
1 *tablespoon soy sauce*
½ *teaspoon salt*
¼ *teaspoon white pepper*
¼ *teaspoon 5-spice powder*
½ *teaspoon sugar*
2 *teaspoons sesame oil*

2 *tablespoons peanut oil*

1 *cup hot water*

1 *tablespoon peanut oil*

TO PREPARE:

Wring out celery cabbage in a clean, dry dish towel to remove excess moisture. Combine filling ingredients in a large bowl

and mix thoroughly. Divide the filling into equal balls containing
1 tablespoon each.

TO ASSEMBLE:

Moisten one side of the skin with water. Place a ball of
filling in the center of the skin. Fold the skin over the filling to
form a half circle. Pinch the edges together. Place the dumplings
on a floured plate, not touching each other, or they will stick.
Cover with a damp dish towel until you are ready to fry them.

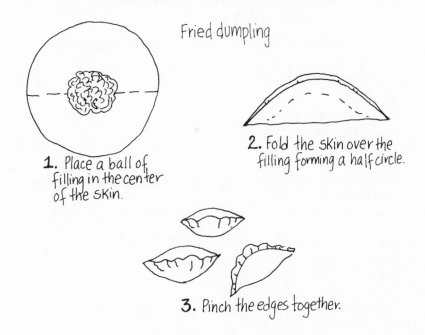

Fried dumpling

1. Place a ball of filling in the center of the skin.

2. Fold the skin over the filling forming a half circle.

3. Pinch the edges together.

TO COOK:

To a heated skillet add 2 tablespoons peanut oil. When oil is
hot, place the dumplings in the skillet with the pinched edge on
top so the bottoms will brown. Turn heat to low and brown the
dumplings about 1 minute. Add 1 cup of hot water to the skillet,
cover, and cook the dumplings about 10 minutes. Uncover skillet,
pour off any water, add 1 tablespoon peanut oil to the skillet and
brown dumplings 1 more minute. Remove from heat and serve
immediately with the Spicy Soy Dipping Sauce.

RICE NOODLES WITH MEAT AND VEGETABLES

PREPARATION TIME: 30 MINUTES   PEKING
COOKING TIME: 10 MINUTES

½ pound rice noodles

½ cup lean, ground pork

½ cup uncooked boneless chicken, shredded

½ cup small uncooked shrimp, shelled, deveined, and
    sliced in half lengthwise

2 tablespoons peanut oil

2 tablespoons peanut oil

SEASONINGS:
½ teaspoon minced fresh ginger
½ teaspoon minced garlic

VEGETABLES:
6 dried Chinese mushrooms, soaked in warm water 30 minutes
½ cup bean sprouts
¼ cup fresh or frozen snow peas, strings and stems removed

SAUCE:
4 tablespoons soy sauce
2 tablespoons dry sherry
½ teaspoon salt
½ teaspoon sugar
¼ teaspoon black pepper

1 whole scallion, thinly sliced

TO PREPARE:
    Place rice noodles in a large mixing bowl. Cover noodles with
boiling water and set aside about 5 minutes until they are soft.
Drain noodles well and place in a large bowl. Rinse mushrooms,
discard tough stems, and shred.

ON THE TRAY:
    Bottle of peanut oil

Cup containing pork
Cup containing chicken
Cup containing shrimp
Cup containing seasonings
Bowl containing vegetables
Bowl containing noodles
Bowl containing sauce
Cup containing scallion

TO COOK:

To a heated wok add 2 tablespoons peanut oil. When oil is hot, add pork and stir-fry about 1 minute until it loses its pink color. Add chicken and stir-fry about 1 minute until it loses its pink color. Add shrimp and stir-fry about 30 seconds, until they turn pink. Remove pork, chicken, and shrimp from the wok and set aside in a bowl.

In the same wok heat 2 tablespoons peanut oil. Add seasonings and stir-fry 30 seconds. Add vegetables and stir-fry 30 seconds. Add noodles and stir to mix thoroughly. Add sauce and stir to mix. Return pork, chicken, and shrimp to the wok and stir well to mix all the ingredients. Remove from heat and garnish with scallion. Serve immediately.

EGG FU YUNG (*makes 6–8 pancakes*)

PREPARATION TIME: 30 MINUTES   CANTON
COOKING TIME: 12 MINUTES

6   *eggs, lightly beaten*

VEGETABLES:
6   *whole scallions, chopped*
2   *dried Chinese mushrooms, soaked in warm water 30 minutes*
1   *celery stalk, finely chopped*
1   *cup coarsely chopped bean sprouts*

1   *cup chopped ham*

½   *teaspoon salt*

¼   *teaspoon white pepper*

1   *teaspoon peanut oil*

½   *teaspoon minced fresh ginger*

SAUCE:
1   *cup canned chicken broth*
1   *tablespoon soy sauce*

2   *teaspoons cornstarch, dissolved in 2 teaspoons cold water*

1   *tablespoon peanut oil*

TO PREPARE:

Rinse mushrooms, discard tough stems, and chop. Combine eggs, vegetables, ham, salt, and pepper in a large mixing bowl.

ON THE TRAY:

Bottle of peanut oil
Cup containing ginger
Cup containing sauce
Cup containing dissolved cornstarch
Bowl containing eggs, vegetables, ham, salt, and pepper

TO COOK:
Step 1:

To a heated saucepan add 1 teaspoon peanut oil. When oil is hot add ginger, stir and add sauce, and bring to a boil. Add cornstarch and stir about 1 minute until the sauce is thickened. Remove from heat.

Step 2:

In a heated skillet add 1 tablespoon peanut oil. When oil is hot, add 2 tablespoons of the egg mixture to make a pancake about 4 inches in diameter. Cook about 30 seconds on one side until it is lightly browned, turn, and cook the other side about 30 seconds. Remove pancake from skillet and keep warm in a low, 200° oven while you make the others. Add more peanut oil if you need to while cooking the remainder of the pancakes.

TO SERVE:

Place pancakes on a platter and serve warm sauce in a separate bowl.

You may substitute shrimp or crabmeat for the ham in this recipe.

BROCCOLI STEM SALAD

PREPARATION TIME: 15 MINUTES   PEKING
CHILLING TIME: 1 HOUR

Stems from 1 bunch of broccoli

DRESSING:
2   *tablespoons soy sauce*
2   *tablespoons sesame oil*
1   *teaspoon white rice vinegar*
½   *teaspoon sugar*

TO PREPARE:
Peel broccoli stems, removing tough strings. Cut stems on a diagonal into 1-inch pieces. Cover and refrigerate. Mix dressing. Combine dressing and broccoli just before serving.

SPICED FRESH LOTUS ROOT SALAD

PREPARATION TIME: 10 MINUTES   SZECHUAN
CHILLING TIME: 1 HOUR

2   *pieces fresh lotus root, 6–8 inches long*

DRESSING:
2   *tablespoons sesame oil*
¼   *teaspoon chili paste with garlic*
1   *tablespoon sugar*
2   *tablespoons white rice vinegar*
2   *tablespoons soy sauce*

TO PREPARE:
Peel lotus root and slice thin. Bring 1 quart of water to a boil and add lotus root. Bring to a boil again and drain. Rinse

lotus root with cold water and dry well on paper towels. Refrigerate. Combine ingredients for the dressing and refrigerate. Combine dressing and lotus root just before serving.

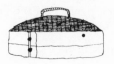

STIR-FRIED ASPARAGUS

PREPARATION TIME: 10 MINUTES   CANTON
COOKING TIME: 4 MINUTES

1   pound fresh asparagus, trimmed and cut into 1-inch pieces

2   tablespoons peanut oil

SAUCE:
1   tablespoon soy sauce
1   tablespoon dry sherry
1   teaspoon salt
1   teaspoon sugar
3   tablespoons water

1   teaspoon cornstarch, dissolved in 2 teaspoons cold water

ON THE TRAY:
Bottle of peanut oil
Bowl containing asparagus
Cup containing sauce
Cup containing dissolved cornstarch

TO COOK:
To a heated wok add 2 tablespoons peanut oil. When the oil is hot, add asparagus and stir-fry 1 minute. Add sauce, cover, and reduce heat to medium. Cook 2 minutes. Remove cover. Add cornstarch and stir about 1 minute until the sauce is thickened. Remove from heat and serve immediately.

This dish can be made with broccoli or cauliflower instead of asparagus.

VEGETABLE CASSEROLE

PREPARATION TIME: 30 MINUTES   PEKING
COOKING TIME: 8 MINUTES

4   cups celery cabbage, cut into 1 × 2-inch rectangles

VEGETABLES:
½ cup sliced canned bamboo shoots
½ cup sliced carrots
½ cup sliced canned water chestnuts
8   dried Chinese mushrooms, soaked in warm water 30 minutes

*2   squares fresh bean curd, sliced into ½-inch pieces
     (optional)*

SAUCE:
2   cups canned chicken broth
1   teaspoon salt
½ teaspoon white pepper

TO PREPARE:
Rinse mushrooms, discard tough stems, and cut in quarters.

ON THE TRAY:
Bowl containing sauce
Bowl containing cabbage
Bowl containing other vegetables
Cup containing bean curd

TO COOK:
Bring sauce to a boil in a flameproof casserole. Add cabbage
and cook 3 minutes. Add other vegetables and cook 3 minutes.
Add bean curd and heat through. Serve in individual bowls from
the casserole or a tureen. Eat vegetables with chopsticks and
drink soup from the bowls.

SHRIMP PEKING

1   *pound (about 24) large shrimp, shelled and deveined*

2   *tablespoons peanut oil*

2   *tablespoons peanut oil*

SEASONINGS:
1   *teaspoon minced fresh ginger*
1   *teaspoon minced garlic*

VEGETABLES:
8   *dried Chinese mushrooms, soaked in warm water 30 minutes*
½ *cup diced canned water chestnuts*
½ *cup diced canned bamboo shoots*
½ *cup fresh or frozen snow peas, stems and strings removed,
     and diced*

SAUCE:
½ *cup canned chicken broth*
2   *tablespoons dry sherry*
1   *tablespoon hoisin sauce*
1   *tablespoon ground brown bean sauce*
1   *teaspoon sugar*
1   *teaspoon salt*

   1   *tablespoon cornstarch, dissolved in 2 tablespoons
        cold water*

TO PREPARE:
Rinse mushrooms, discard tough stems, and dice.

ON THE TRAY:
Bottle of peanut oil
Bowl containing shrimp
Cup containing seasonings
Bowl containing vegetables
Bowl containing sauce
Cup containing dissolved cornstarch

TO COOK:

To a heated wok add 2 tablespoons peanut oil. When oil is hot add shrimp. Stir-fry about 1 minute until they turn pink. Remove shrimp from the wok and set aside in a bowl.

In the same wok heat 2 tablespoons peanut oil. Add seasonings and stir-fry 30 seconds. Add vegetables and stir-fry 1 minute. Add sauce and stir until it boils. Add shrimp and stir-fry 30 seconds. Add dissolved cornstarch and stir about 1 minute until thickened. Remove from heat and serve immediately.

SHRIMP, HAM, AND BROCCOLI

PREPARATION TIME: 30 MINUTES   PEKING
COOKING TIME: 5 MINUTES

½ pound (about 12) large shrimp, shelled, deveined, and
     cut in half lengthwise

¼ pound ham, cut into slices ¼ × 1 × 1 inch

2 tablespoons peanut oil

2 tablespoons peanut oil

½ teaspoon minced garlic

VEGETABLES:
1   cup broccoli flowers
½ cup fresh or frozen snow peas, strings and stems removed
6   dried Chinese mushrooms, soaked in warm water 30 minutes
½ cup sliced carrots

SAUCE:
½ cup canned chicken broth
1   teaspoon salt
½ teaspoon sugar
2   tablespoons dry sherry

2   teaspoons cornstarch, dissolved in 2 teaspoons cold water

TO PREPARE:

Rinse mushrooms, discard tough stems, and cut in half.

Bring 1 quart of water to a boil. Add broccoli and carrots and bring to a boil again. Cover and cook 3 minutes. Drain and rinse in cold water.

ON THE TRAY:
> Bottle of peanut oil
> Bowl containing shrimp
> Cup containing garlic
> Bowl containing vegetables
> Cup containing sauce
> Cup containing ham
> Cup containing dissolved cornstarch

TO COOK:

To a heated wok add 2 tablespoons peanut oil. When oil is hot add shrimp and stir-fry 1 minute until they turn pink. Remove shrimp and set aside in a bowl.

In the same wok heat 2 tablespoons peanut oil. Add garlic and stir. Add vegetables and stir-fry 1 minute. Add sauce and stir until it comes to a boil. Return shrimp to the wok and add ham. Stir to heat through. Add cornstarch and stir 1 minute until sauce is thickened. Remove from heat and serve immediately.

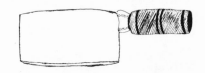

SHRIMP AND VEGETABLES

PREPARATION TIME: 30 MINUTES   CANTON
COOKING TIME: 8 MINUTES

1   *pound (about 24) large shrimp, shelled and deveined*

2   *tablespoons peanut oil*

2   *tablespoons peanut oil*

½   *teaspoon minced garlic*

½   *cup carrots, thinly sliced on a diagonal*

VEGETABLES:

8   *dried Chinese mushrooms, soaked in warm water 30 minutes*
½   *cup canned baby ears of corn, drained and cut in half*
    lengthwise
½   *cup sliced canned water chestnuts*
½   *cup fresh or frozen snow peas, stems and strings removed*

SAUCE:

½   *cup canned chicken broth*
2   *tablespoons dry sherry*
1   *teaspoon salt*
½   *teaspoon sugar*

    2   *teaspoons cornstarch, dissolved in 2 teaspoons cold water*

TO PREPARE:

Rinse mushrooms, discard tough stems, and cut in half.

ON THE TRAY:

Bottle of peanut oil
Bowl containing shrimp
Cup containing garlic
Cup containing carrots
Bowl containing vegetables
Bowl containing sauce
Cup containing dissolved cornstarch

TO COOK:

To a heated wok add 2 tablespoons peanut oil. When the oil is hot, add shrimp and stir-fry about 1 minute until they turn pink. Remove shrimp and set aside in a bowl.

In the same wok heat 2 tablespoons peanut oil and add garlic. Stir-fry 30 seconds. Add carrots and stir-fry 1 minute. Add vegetables and stir-fry 1 minute. Add sauce and stir until it boils. Return shrimp to wok and stir 30 seconds. Add cornstarch and stir until sauce is thickened, about 1 minute. Remove from heat and serve immediately.

SHRIMP WITH PINE NUTS

PREPARATION TIME: 20 MINUTES   PEKING
MARINATING TIME: 30 MINUTES
COOKING TIME: 5 MINUTES

1 *pound (about 48–50) small shrimp, shelled and*
   deveined

MARINADE:
1 *egg*
½ *teaspoon salt*
¼ *teaspoon white pepper*
3 *tablespoons cornstarch*

   3 *tablespoons peanut oil*

   2 *tablespoons peanut oil*

SEASONINGS:
1 *teaspoon minced fresh ginger*
1 *teaspoon minced garlic*
½ *cup chopped onion*

SAUCE:
¾ *cup canned chicken broth*
2 *teaspoons sugar*
½ *teaspoon salt*
4 *tablespoons catsup*
2 *tablespoons dry sherry*

   ½ *cup pine nuts*

   1 *whole scallion, thinly sliced*

TO PREPARE:
   Combine ingredients for marinade and mix until smooth.
Add shrimp and set aside for 30 minutes.

ON THE TRAY:
   Bottle of peanut oil
   Bowl containing shrimp in marinade
   Cup containing seasonings

Bowl containing sauce
Cup containing pine nuts
Cup containing scallion

TO COOK:

To a heated wok add 3 tablespoons peanut oil. When oil is hot, add shrimp and stir-fry about 1 minute until they turn pink. Remove shrimp from the wok and set aside in a bowl.

In the same wok heat 2 tablespoons peanut oil. Add seasonings and stir-fry 30 seconds. Add sauce and stir until it boils. Return shrimp to wok and stir. Add pine nuts and stir. Remove from heat and garnish with scallion. Serve immediately.

BATTER-DIPPED CRABMEAT

PREPARATION TIME: 10 MINUTES   CANTON
MARINATING TIME: 30 MINUTES
COOKING TIME: 15 MINUTES

1   *pound fresh king crabmeat, shelled and cut into 2-inch
    lengths*

MARINADE:
2   *tablespoons dry sherry*
½   *teaspoon minced fresh ginger*
½   *teaspoon minced garlic*

BATTER:
½   *cup all-purpose flour*
1   *teaspoon baking powder*
1   *teaspoon salt*
2   *tablespoons peanut oil*
½   *cup ice water*

4   *cups peanut oil for deep frying*

4   *large lettuce leaves*

1   *lemon, sliced*

Roasted salt and pepper (optional—see recipe)

TO PREPARE:

Combine crab pieces with marinade and set aside for 30 minutes. Combine ingredients for batter and mix until smooth.

TO COOK:

Heat oil to 400° in a deep-fat fryer. Dip crab pieces in batter and fry 6 pieces at a time for 2 minutes until golden brown. Drain on paper towels. Reserve cooking oil in a covered jar to be reused.

TO SERVE:

Arrange lettuce leaves on a platter. Place the crab pieces on top and garnish with lemon slices. Serve with Roasted Salt and Pepper. This is optional.

KING CRABMEAT AND BROCCOLI

PREPARATION TIME: 15 MINUTES   PEKING
COOKING TIME: 5 MINUTES

½ *pound cooked king crabmeat, cut into 2-inch pieces*

1 *bunch broccoli, cut into bite-sized pieces*

2 *tablespoons peanut oil*

½ *teaspoon minced garlic*

SAUCE:
½ *cup canned chicken broth*
½ *teaspoon salt*
2 *tablespoons dry sherry*
¼ *teaspoon sugar*

2 *teaspoons cornstarch, dissolved in 2 teaspoons cold water*

TO PREPARE:

Bring 2 quarts of water to a boil. Add broccoli and bring to a boil again. Cover and cook 2 minutes. Drain and rinse in cold water.

ON THE TRAY:

Bottle of peanut oil
Cup containing garlic
Bowl containing broccoli
Bowl containing crabmeat
Cup containing sauce
Cup containing dissolved cornstarch

TO COOK:

To a heated wok add 2 tablespoons peanut oil. When oil is
hot, add garlic and stir. Add broccoli and stir-fry 1 minute. Add
crabmeat and stir. Add sauce and stir until it comes to a boil.
Add cornstarch and stir 1 minute until the sauce is thickened.
Remove from heat and serve immediately.

SEAFOOD TRIPLE DELIGHT

PREPARATION TIME: 30 MINUTES   SZECHUAN
MARINATING TIME: 30 MINUTES
COOKING TIME: 5 MINUTES

1   *cup medium shrimp, shelled, deveined, and sliced in
    half lengthwise*

MARINADE:

1   *egg white*
1   *tablespoon cornstarch*

2   *tablespoons peanut oil*

2   *tablespoons peanut oil*

SEASONINGS:

1   *teaspoon minced fresh ginger*
1   *teaspoon minced garlic*
1   *whole scallion, minced*

VEGETABLES:

2   *tablespoons tree ears, soaked in warm water 30 minutes*
½   *cup sliced canned water chestnuts*
½   *cup diced red or green sweet pepper*

SAUCE:

¼ cup canned chicken broth
2 tablespoons dry sherry
1 tablespoon white rice vinegar
3 tablespoons soy sauce
½ teaspoon chili paste with garlic
1 teaspoon sugar

1 cup cubed cooked lobster meat

1 cup cubed cooked crabmeat

1 tablespoon cornstarch, dissolved in 2 tablespoons
cold water

1 tablespoon sesame oil (optional)

TO PREPARE:

Combine ingredients for marinade and mix until smooth. Add shrimp and marinate 30 minutes. Rinse tree ears to remove sand, and dice.

ON THE TRAY:

Bottle of peanut oil
Cup containing marinated shrimp
Cup containing seasonings
Cup containing vegetables
Bowl containing sauce
Bowl containing lobster and crabmeat
Cup containing dissolved cornstarch
Bottle of sesame oil

TO COOK:

To a heated wok add 2 tablespoons peanut oil. When oil is hot, add shrimp and stir-fry 30 seconds until they turn pink. Remove shrimp and set aside in a bowl.

In the same wok heat 2 tablespoons peanut oil and add seasonings. Stir-fry 30 seconds. Add vegetables and stir-fry 1 minute. Add sauce and stir until it boils. Add lobster and crabmeat and stir. Return shrimp to wok and stir. Add cornstarch and stir until sauce is thickened. Stir in sesame oil, if desired. Remove from heat and serve immediately.

SHELLED LOBSTER IN SPICY SAUCE

PREPARATION TIME: 15 MINUTES   SZECHUAN
COOKING TIME: 5 MINUTES

> 2   cups cooked lobster meat, cut into 1-inch cubes
>
> 2   tablespoons peanut oil

SEASONINGS:
1   teaspoon minced fresh ginger
1   teaspoon minced garlic
¼   cup chopped onion

SAUCE:
¼   cup canned chicken broth
2   tablespoons catsup
2   tablespoons dry sherry
1   teaspoon chili paste with garlic
1   teaspoon sugar
½   teaspoon salt

> ¼   cup frozen peas, thawed
>
> 1   teaspoon cornstarch, dissolved in 2 teaspoons cold water
>
> 1   teaspoon sesame oil (optional)
>
> 1   whole scallion, thinly sliced

ON THE TRAY:
Bottle of peanut oil
Cup containing seasonings
Cup containing sauce
Bowl containing lobster meat
Cup containing peas
Cup containing dissolved cornstarch
Bottle of sesame oil
Cup containing scallion

TO COOK:
To a heated wok add 2 tablespoons peanut oil. When oil is hot, add seasonings and stir-fry 30 seconds. Add sauce and stir

until it boils. Add lobster meat and peas and stir. Add cornstarch
and stir about 1 minute until the sauce is thickened. Stir in sesame
oil, if desired. Remove from heat and garnish with scallion. Serve
immediately.

SWEET AND PUNGENT FISH

PREPARATION TIME: 20 MINUTES   CANTON
MARINATING TIME: 10 MINUTES
COOKING TIME: 10 MINUTES

   1   *pound fish filets, flounder or sole, cut into 1 × 2-inch*
      pieces

MARINADE:
3   *tablespoons dry sherry*
½   *teaspoon salt*

BATTER:
½   *cup flour*
¼   *cup cornstarch*
1   *teaspoon baking powder*
¾   *cup water*
1   *tablespoon peanut oil*

   4   *cups peanut oil for deep-fat frying*

   3   *tablespoons peanut oil*

SEASONINGS:
½   *teaspoon minced fresh ginger*
¼   *cup chopped onion*

VEGETABLES:
1   *small carrot, thinly sliced*
¼   *cup diced sweet green pepper*

SAUCE:
⅔   *cup canned chicken broth*
½   *cup white rice vinegar*
½   *cup sugar*
2   *tablespoons soy sauce*

½ cup canned pineapple chunks, drained

2 tablespoons cornstarch, dissolved in 2 tablespoons cold water

TO PREPARE:

Combine fish pieces in marinade and set aside 10 minutes. Combine ingredients for batter and mix until smooth. Add fish pieces to the batter.

ON THE TRAY:

Bottle of peanut oil
Bowl containing fish pieces in batter
Cup containing seasonings
Cup containing vegetables
Bowl containing sauce
Cup containing pineapple
Cup containing dissolved cornstarch

TO COOK:

Step 1:

Heat 4 cups peanut oil to 375° in a deep-fat fryer. Fry fish a few pieces at a time for about 2 minutes until golden. Drain on paper towels. Fish may be kept warm in a low, 200° oven until the sauce is ready. Reserve cooking oil in a covered jar to be reused.

Step 2:

To a heated wok add 3 tablespoons peanut oil. When oil is hot, add seasonings and stir-fry 30 seconds. Add vegetables and stir-fry 30 seconds. Add sauce and stir until it boils. Add pineapple chunks and stir. Add cornstarch and stir about 1 minute until the sauce is thickened. Remove from heat.

TO SERVE:

Place fried fish pieces on a large, deep platter. Pour the sauce over the fish. Serve immediately.

This recipe can be made using shrimp instead of fish filets.

DEEP-FRIED FISH WITH HUNAN SAUCE

PREPARATION TIME: 30 MINUTES   HUNAN
COOKING TIME: 12 MINUTES

  1 *2-pound whole white fish, such as sole, flounder, or
     sea bass*

    Cornstarch

  4 *cups peanut oil for deep-fat frying*

  3 *tablespoons peanut oil*

SEASONINGS:
1 *teaspoon minced fresh ginger*
½ *teaspoon minced garlic*

VEGETABLES:
4 *dried Chinese mushrooms, soaked in warm water 30 minutes*
½ *cup chopped canned bamboo shoots*
½ *cup chopped red or green sweet pepper*

SAUCE:
1½ *cups canned chicken broth*
4 *tablespoons soy sauce*
1 *teaspoon hoisin sauce*
1 *teaspoon sugar*
½ *teaspoon chili paste with garlic*

    2 *tablespoons cornstarch, dissolved in 2 tablespoons
       cold water*

    1 *tablespoon sesame oil (optional)*

    1 *whole scallion, thinly sliced*

TO PREPARE:
Make 3 deep, diagonal cuts from the backbone toward the tail on each side of the fish. Dredge the fish in cornstarch, making sure it gets inside the cuts. Rinse mushrooms, discard tough stems, and chop.

ON THE TRAY:
Bottle of peanut oil

Platter containing fish dredged in cornstarch
Cup containing seasonings
Bowl containing vegetables
Bowl containing sauce
Cup containing dissolved cornstarch
Bottle of sesame oil
Cup containing scallion

TO COOK:
Step 1:
Heat 4 cups of peanut oil to 375° in a wok or large pot. Add fish gently and fry 4 minutes on each side. Remove fish from oil and drain on paper towels. Fish may be kept warm in a low, 200° oven while you are making the sauce. Reserve the cooking oil in a covered jar to be reused.

Step 2:
To a heated wok add 3 tablespoons of peanut oil. When oil is hot, add seasonings and stir. Add vegetables and stir-fry 30 seconds. Add sauce and stir until it boils. Add cornstarch dissolved in water and stir about 1 minute until the sauce thickens. Stir in sesame oil, if desired, and remove from heat.

TO SERVE:
Place fish on a large, deep platter. Pour sauce over the fish. Garnish with scallion. Serve immediately.

BEEF WITH SPINACH

PREPARATION TIME: 20 MINUTES   PEKING
MARINATING TIME: 30 MINUTES
COOKING TIME: 5 MINUTES

1   *pound flank steak, thinly sliced across the grain,*
    ¼ inch thick × 2 inches long

MARINADE:
1 egg
1 tablespoon cornstarch
½ teaspoon salt
1 tablespoon peanut oil

   3 tablespoons peanut oil

   2 tablespoons peanut oil

SEASONINGS:
1 teaspoon minced fresh ginger
1 teaspoon minced garlic
1 whole scallion, minced

SAUCE:
¼ cup canned chicken broth
1 tablespoon dry sherry
3 tablespoons soy sauce
1 teaspoon sugar

   1 teaspoon cornstarch, dissolved in 2 teaspoons cold water

   1 pound fresh spinach, washed and trimmed

   1 cup water

TO PREPARE:
   Combine ingredients for marinade and mix until smooth.
Add beef and marinate 30 minutes. Bring cup of water to a boil.
Add spinach and stir about 1 minute just until it is wilted. Drain.
Place in colander over boiling water to keep warm.

ON THE TRAY:
   Bottle of peanut oil
   Bowl containing marinated beef
   Cup containing seasonings
   Cup containing sauce
   Cup containing dissolved cornstarch

TO COOK:
   To a heated wok add 3 tablespoons peanut oil. When oil is
hot, add beef and stir-fry about 2 minutes until it loses its pink
color. Remove beef from wok and set aside in a bowl.

In the same wok heat 2 tablespoons peanut oil and add seasonings. Stir-fry 30 seconds. Add sauce and stir until it boils. Return beef to wok and stir. Add cornstarch and stir about 1 minute until sauce is thickened. Remove from heat.

TO SERVE:

Arrange spinach on a large, deep platter. Place beef and sauce on top. Serve immediately.

BEEF PEKING

PREPARATION TIME: 15 MINUTES   PEKING
MARINATING TIME: 30 MINUTES
COOKING TIME: 5 MINUTES

1 *pound flank steak, thinly sliced across the grain and shredded*

MARINADE:
1 *egg*
1 *teaspoon dry sherry*
½ *teaspoon salt*
1 *tablespoon cornstarch*
1 *tablespoon peanut oil*

2 *tablespoons peanut oil*

2 *tablespoons peanut oil*

2 *tablespoons shredded fresh ginger*

SAUCE:
3 *tablespoons hoisin sauce*
2 *tablespoons dry sherry*
3 *tablespoons soy sauce*
½ *teaspoon sugar*
1 *tablespoon water*

½ *teaspoon cornstarch, dissolved in 1 teaspoon cold water*

7 *whole scallions, cut into 2-inch lengths and shredded*

TO PREPARE:

Combine ingredients for marinade and mix until smooth. Add beef and marinate 30 minutes.

ON THE TRAY:

Bottle of peanut oil
Bowl containing marinated beef
Cup containing ginger
Bowl containing sauce
Cup containing dissolved cornstarch
Cup containing scallions

TO COOK:

To a heated wok add 2 tablespoons peanut oil. When oil is hot, add beef and stir-fry about 2 minutes until it loses its pink color. Remove beef from wok and set aside in a bowl.

In the same wok heat 2 tablespoons peanut oil. Add ginger and stir-fry 30 seconds. Add sauce and stir until it boils. Return beef to the sauce. Add cornstarch and stir about 1 minute until the sauce thickens. Remove from heat and garnish with scallions. Serve immediately.

SPICY SHREDDED GARLIC BEEF

PREPARATION TIME: 30 MINUTES   SZECHUAN
MARINATING TIME: 30 MINUTES
COOKING TIME: 8 MINUTES

½ pound flank steak, thinly sliced across the grain and shredded

MARINADE:
1 egg
1 teaspoon dry sherry
1 tablespoon peanut oil
½ teaspoon salt

2 tablespoons peanut oil

2 tablespoons peanut oil

SEASONINGS:

½ teaspoon minced fresh ginger
1 teaspoon minced garlic

VEGETABLES:

2 tablespoons tree ears, soaked in warm water 30 minutes
¼ cup shredded canned bamboo shoots
½ cup shredded red or green sweet pepper
½ cup sliced canned water chestnuts

SAUCE:

½ cup canned chicken broth
2 tablespoons dry sherry
4 tablespoons soy sauce
1 teaspoon chili paste with garlic
1 teaspoon sugar
1 tablespoon white rice vinegar

   2 teaspoons cornstarch, dissolved in 1 tablespoon cold water

   1 whole scallion, thinly sliced

TO PREPARE:

Combine ingredients for marinade and mix until smooth.
Add beef and marinate 30 minutes. Rinse tree ears to remove
any sand, and shred.

ON THE TRAY:

Bottle of peanut oil
Bowl containing marinated beef
Cup containing seasonings
Bowl containing vegetables
Cup containing sauce
Cup containing dissolved cornstarch
Cup containing scallion

TO COOK:

To a heated wok add 2 tablespoons peanut oil. When oil is
hot, add beef and stir-fry about 2 minutes until it loses its pink
color. Remove beef from the wok and set aside in a bowl.

In the same wok heat 2 tablespoons peanut oil and add
seasonings. Stir-fry 30 seconds. Add vegetables and stir-fry 1

minute. Add sauce and stir until it boils. Return beef to wok and stir. Add cornstarch and stir about 1 minute until the sauce is thickened. Remove from heat and garnish with scallion. Serve immediately.

KUNG PAO LAMB WITH PEANUTS

PREPARATION TIME: 20 MINUTES   SZECHUAN
MARINATING TIME: 30 MINUTES
COOKING TIME: 5 MINUTES

1   *pound lean, boneless lamb, thinly sliced ¼ × 1 × 2 inches*

MARINADE:
1   *egg*
1   *tablespoon cornstarch*
1   *tablespoon peanut oil*
½   *teaspoon salt*
1   *teaspoon dry sherry*

2   *tablespoons peanut oil*

2   *tablespoons peanut oil*

5   *dried red chili peppers, cut in half*

SEASONINGS:
5   *thin slices fresh ginger, ⅛ inch thick × 1 inch diameter*
1   *teaspoon minced garlic*
4   *whole scallions, cut into 1-inch pieces*

SAUCE:
4   *tablespoons dry sherry*
1   *teaspoon sugar*
2   *tablespoons soy sauce*
¼   *cup canned chicken broth*

1   *tablespoon cornstarch, dissolved in 2 tablespoons cold water*

½   *cup unsalted, roasted peanuts*

1   *teaspoon sesame oil (optional)*

TO PREPARE:

Combine ingredients for marinade and mix until smooth. Add lamb and marinate 30 minutes.

ON THE TRAY:

Bottle of peanut oil
Bowl containing marinated lamb
Cup containing dried peppers
Cup containing seasonings
Cup containing sauce
Cup containing dissolved cornstarch
Cup containing peanuts
Bottle of sesame oil

TO COOK:

To a heated wok add 2 tablespoons peanut oil. When oil is hot, add lamb and stir-fry about 2 minutes until lamb loses its pink color. Remove lamb from wok and set aside.

In the same wok heat 2 tablespoons peanut oil and add dried peppers. Stir-fry about 30 seconds until they turn black. Add seasonings and stir. Add sauce and stir until it boils. Return lamb to wok and stir. Add cornstarch and stir sauce until it is thickened. Stir in peanuts. Stir in sesame oil, if desired. Remove from heat and discard dried peppers and ginger slices. Serve immediately.

PORK WITH VEGETABLES AND CASHEWS

PREPARATION TIME: 30 MINUTES   PEKING
MARINATING TIME: 30 MINUTES
COOKING TIME: 8 MINUTES

1   *pound boneless loin of pork, cut into slices*
    ½ × 1 × 1 inch

MARINADE:

2 tablespoons cornstarch
1 egg white
1 teaspoon salt
2 tablespoons peanut oil
¼ teaspoon white pepper

   3 tablespoons peanut oil

   2 tablespoons peanut oil

SEASONINGS:

1 teaspoon minced fresh ginger
1 teaspoon minced garlic
2 whole scallions, minced

VEGETABLES:

½ cup diced red or green sweet pepper
½ cup diced broccoli flowers
¼ cup diced canned bamboo shoots
6 dried Chinese mushrooms, soaked in warm water 30 minutes

SAUCE:

3 tablespoons soy sauce
1 tablespoon dry sherry
1 tablespoon oyster sauce
1 teaspoon hoisin sauce
¼ cup canned chicken broth
1 teaspoon sugar
½ teaspoon salt

   1 teaspoon cornstarch, dissolved in 2 teaspoons cold water

   ½ cup roasted cashew nuts, unsalted

TO PREPARE:

Combine ingredients for marinade and mix until smooth. Add pork and marinate 30 minutes. Rinse mushrooms, discard tough stems, and dice.

ON THE TRAY:

   Bottle of peanut oil
   Bowl containing marinated pork
   Cup containing seasonings

Bowl containing vegetables
Cup containing sauce
Cup containing dissolved cornstarch
Cup containing cashew nuts

TO COOK:

To a heated wok add 3 tablespoons peanut oil. When the oil is hot, add pork and stir-fry about 3 minutes until the pork loses its pink color. Remove pork from the wok and set aside.

In the same wok heat 2 tablespoons of peanut oil and add the seasonings. Stir-fry 30 seconds. Add vegetables and stir-fry 1 minute. Add sauce and stir until it boils. Return pork to wok and stir. Add cornstarch and stir sauce about 1 minute until it is thickened. Stir in cashew nuts. Remove from heat and serve immediately.

PORK WITH SCALLION SAUCE

PREPARATION TIME: 10 MINUTES   FUKIEN
MARINATING TIME: 1 HOUR
COOKING TIME: 15 MINUTES

1   pound boneless pork tenderloin, cut into slices ½ inch
    thick × 2 inches square

MARINADE:
1   teaspoon soy sauce
1   teaspoon dry sherry
1   teaspoon sesame oil
½   teaspoon 5-spice powder
½   teaspoon salt
½   teaspoon sugar

    Cornstarch

4   cups peanut oil for deep frying

SAUCE:
3   tablespoons soy sauce
4   tablespoons white rice vinegar
4   tablespoons sugar
½   teaspoon salt

6   *whole scallions, thinly sliced*

TO PREPARE:

Combine ingredients for marinade, add pork slices, and set aside for 1 hour. Dredge pork in cornstarch.

ON THE TRAY:

Bottle of peanut oil
Platter containing pork slices
Cup containing sauce
Cup containing scallions

TO COOK:

Step 1:

Heat 4 cups peanut oil to 375° in a deep-fat fryer. Fry pork 6 slices at a time, about 4 minutes until golden brown. Drain on paper towels. Keep pork warm in a low, 200° oven while you prepare the sauce. Reserve cooking oil in a covered jar to be reused.

Step 2:

Heat combined sauce ingredients in a saucepan just to boiling. Add scallions and stir. Add pork slices. Remove from heat and serve immediately.

ROAST PORK WITH VEGETABLES

PREPARATION TIME: 30 MINUTES   CANTON
COOKING TIME: 5 MINUTES

½   *pound Chinese roast pork, sliced ½ × 1 × 1 inch*

3   *tablespoons peanut oil*

½   *teaspoon minced fresh ginger*
¼   *cup carrots, thinly sliced on a diagonal*
1   *cup sliced broccoli flowers*

SAUCE:
¾ cup canned chicken broth
1   tablespoon dry sherry
3   tablespoons soy sauce
1   teaspoon sugar

VEGETABLES:
6   dried Chinese mushrooms, soaked in warm water 30 minutes
½ cup fresh or frozen snow peas, strings and stems removed
¼ cup sliced canned water chestnuts
½ cup canned baby ears of corn, drained and sliced in half
    lengthwise

    1   tablespoon cornstarch, dissolved in 2 tablespoons
        cold water

TO PREPARE:
    Rinse mushrooms, discard tough stems, and slice.

ON THE TRAY:
    Bottle of peanut oil
    Cup containing ginger
    Bowl containing carrots and broccoli
    Cup containing sauce
    Bowl containing vegetables
    Bowl containing roast pork
    Cup containing dissolved cornstarch

TO COOK:
    To a heated wok add 3 tablespoons peanut oil. When oil is
hot, add ginger and stir. Add carrots and broccoli and stir-fry
1 minute. Add sauce, bring to a boil, and cook carrots and broccoli
2 minutes. Add vegetables and pork and stir. Add cornstarch and
stir about 1 minute until the sauce is thickened. Remove from
heat and serve immediately.

GARLIC PORK WITH VEGETABLES

PREPARATION TIME: 30 MINUTES   SZECHUAN
MARINATING TIME: 30 MINUTES
COOKING TIME: 8 MINUTES

> ½ *pound lean pork tenderloin, shredded*

MARINADE:
1 *egg*
1 *tablespoon peanut oil*
1 *tablespoon dry sherry*
¼ *teaspoon salt*

   2 *tablespoons peanut oil*

   2 *tablespoons peanut oil*

SEASONINGS:
1 *teaspoon minced garlic*
1 *teaspoon minced ginger*

VEGETABLES:
2 *tablespoons tree ears, soaked in warm water 30 minutes*
½ *cup fresh or frozen snow peas, stems and strings removed, and shredded*
½ *cup shredded sweet red pepper*
8 *canned water chestnuts, sliced*
½ *cup shredded canned bamboo shoots*

SAUCE:
½ *cup canned chicken broth* ˙
2 *tablespoons dry sherry*
3 *tablespoons soy sauce*
1 *teaspoon chili paste with garlic*
1 *teaspoon sugar*
1 *tablespoon white rice vinegar*

   2 *teaspoons cornstarch, dissolved in 2 teaspoons cold water*

TO PREPARE:
Rinse tree ears to remove any sand, and shred. Combine

ingredients for marinade and mix until smooth. Add pork and marinate 30 minutes.

ON THE TRAY:

Bottle of peanut oil
Bowl containing marinated pork
Cup containing seasonings
Bowl containing vegetables
Cup containing sauce
Cup containing dissolved cornstarch

TO COOK:

To a heated wok add 2 tablespoons peanut oil. When oil is hot, add marinated pork and stir-fry 3 minutes until the pork loses its pink color. Remove the pork from the wok and set aside.

In the same wok heat 2 tablespoons peanut oil. Add seasonings and stir-fry 30 seconds. Add vegetables and stir-fry 1 minute. Add sauce and stir until it boils. Return pork to the wok and stir to heat through. Add cornstarch and stir about 1 minute until it is thickened. Remove from heat and serve immediately.

HONEY-DIPPED DRUMSTICKS

PREPARATION TIME: 5 MINUTES   CANTON
MARINATING TIME: 6 HOURS OR OVERNIGHT
COOKING TIME: 20 MINUTES

12 *chicken drumsticks (without thighs)*

MARINADE:
¼ *cup honey*
¼ *cup soy sauce*
2 *tablespoons white rice vinegar*
1 *tablespoon brown sugar*

4 *tablespoons flour*
¼ *teaspoon salt*

4 *cups peanut oil for deep frying*

TO PREPARE:

Combine ingredients for marinade. Marinate drumsticks at room temperature 6 hours, or overnight in the refrigerator. Remove drumsticks from marinade and roll in flour and salt combined.

TO COOK:

Heat 4 cups of peanut oil to 375° in a deep-fat fryer. Fry 6 drumsticks at a time, about 8–10 minutes until golden brown. Drain on paper towels. Reserve cooking oil in a covered jar to be reused. Serve immediately.

CHICKEN PEKING

PREPARATION TIME: 20 MINUTES   PEKING
MARINATING TIME: 30 MINUTES
COOKING TIME: 6–8 MINUTES

2   *whole chicken breasts, boned, skinned, and cut into
½-inch cubes*

MARINADE:
1   *egg white*
1   *tablespoon cornstarch*
1   *tablespoon peanut oil*
½   *teaspoon salt*
¼   *teaspoon white pepper*

3   *tablespoons peanut oil*

2   *tablespoons peanut oil*

1   *teaspoon minced fresh ginger*

VEGETABLES:
¼   *cup sliced fresh or canned mushrooms*
¼   *cup diced red sweet pepper*

SAUCE:
¼ cup canned chicken broth
2 tablespoons soy sauce
2 tablespoons dry sherry
2 tablespoons hoisin sauce

1 teaspoon cornstarch, dissolved in 2 teaspoons cold water

TO PREPARE:
Combine ingredients for marinade and mix until smooth.
Add the chicken and marinate 30 minutes.

ON THE TRAY:
Bottle of peanut oil
Bowl containing marinated chicken
Cup containing ginger
Cup containing vegetables
Cup containing sauce
Cup containing dissolved cornstarch

TO COOK:
To a heated wok add 3 tablespoons peanut oil. When the oil
is hot, add chicken and stir-fry about 2 minutes until it loses its
pink color. Remove chicken from wok and set aside in a bowl.
In the same wok heat 2 tablespoons peanut oil, add ginger,
and stir-fry 30 seconds. Add vegetables and stir-fry 1 minute. Add
sauce and stir until it boils. Return chicken to wok and stir.
Add cornstarch and stir about 1 minute until the sauce is thickened. Remove from heat and serve immediately.

TRIPLE FRAGRANCE

PREPARATION TIME: 30 MINUTES   SZECHUAN
MARINATING TIME: 30 MINUTES
COOKING TIME: 6 MINUTES

½ cup lean boneless pork, shredded
½ cup chicken breast, boned, skinned, and shredded

½ cup medium shrimp, shelled, deveined, and sliced in
half lengthwise

MARINADE:
2 egg whites
1 teaspoon salt
3 tablespoons cornstarch
2 tablespoons peanut oil

    3 tablespoons peanut oil

    2 tablespoons peanut oil

SEASONINGS:
½ teaspoon minced fresh ginger
½ teaspoon minced garlic

VEGETABLES:
½ cup shredded canned bamboo shoots
2 tablespoons tree ears, soaked in warm water 30 minutes
½ sweet red or green pepper, shredded
8 canned water chestnuts, sliced

SAUCE:
½ cup canned chicken broth
2 tablespoons dry sherry
2 tablespoons soy sauce
1 teaspoon chili paste with garlic
1 teaspoon sugar
1 tablespoon white rice vinegar

    1 teaspoon cornstarch, dissolved in 2 teaspoons cold water

    1 teaspoon sesame oil (optional)

    1 whole scallion, thinly sliced

TO PREPARE:
    Combine ingredients for marinade and mix until smooth.
Marinate the pork, chicken, and shrimp in separate bowls for 30
minutes. Rinse tree ears to remove sand, and shred.

ON THE TRAY:
    Bottle of peanut oil
    Cup containing marinated pork

Cup containing marinated chicken
Cup containing marinated shrimp
Cup containing seasonings
Bowl containing vegetables
Cup containing sauce
Cup containing dissolved cornstarch
Bottle of sesame oil
Cup containing scallion

TO COOK:

To a heated wok add 3 tablespoons peanut oil. When oil is hot, add pork and stir-fry 1 minute. Add chicken and stir-fry pork and chicken 1 minute, until they lose their pink color. Add shrimp and stir-fry 1 minute or until shrimp turn pink. Remove pork, chicken, and shrimp from wok and set aside in a bowl.

In the same wok heat 2 tablespoons peanut oil and add the seasonings. Stir-fry 30 seconds. Add the vegetables and stir-fry 30 seconds. Add sauce and bring to a boil. When sauce comes to a boil, return pork, chicken, and shrimp to the wok. Add cornstarch and stir about 1 minute until the sauce is thickened. Stir in sesame oil, if desired. Remove from heat and garnish with scallion. Serve immediately.

MANDARIN INN-STYLE ROAST DUCK

PREPARATION TIME: 12 HOURS   PEKING
COOKING TIME: 1 HOUR 50 MINUTES

1   *5-pound duck, thawed*

Boiling water

1   *cup honey*

2   *tablespoons peanut oil*

2   *tablespoons minced fresh ginger*

SAUCE:

2   cups canned chicken broth
3   tablespoons soy sauce
1   tablespoon oyster sauce
2   tablespoons dry sherry
1   teaspoon sugar

   ½   cup sliced fresh or canned mushrooms

   2   tablespoons cornstarch, dissolved in 2 tablespoons
     cold water

   1   tablespoon sesame oil (optional)

TO PREPARE:

Prepare the duck by plunging it into boiling water 3 times as described in the recipe for Peking Duck. Hang duck in a cool place for 12 hours, then refrigerate until you are ready to roast it.

ON THE TRAY:

Bottle of peanut oil
Cup containing ginger
Cup containing sauce
Cup containing mushrooms
Cup containing dissolved cornstarch
Bottle of sesame oil

TO COOK:

Step 1:

Heat oven to 350°. Place duck breast down on rack in a roasting pan. Add 1 inch of boiling water in the bottom of the roasting pan. *Do not let the duck touch the water.* Roast the duck for 1 hour and 45 minutes, turning the duck 3 times for even cooking. Let the duck cool slightly.

Step 2:

To a heated wok add 2 tablespoons peanut oil. When the oil is hot, add ginger and stir-fry 30 seconds. Add sauce and stir until it boils. Add mushrooms and stir. Add cornstarch and stir about 1 minute until the sauce thickens. Stir in sesame oil, if desired. Remove from heat.

TO SERVE:

With a cleaver chop duck up into bite-sized pieces, bones and all, and arrange on a platter to resemble a whole duck. Pour sauce over the duck. Serve immediately.

PINEAPPLE DUCK

PREPARATION TIME: 5 MINUTES   CANTON
COOKING TIME: 3 MINUTES

2   cups cooked duck meat (See preceding recipe for roast duck.)

2   tablespoons peanut oil

1   cup chopped onions

SAUCE:
1   cup pineapple juice drained from the canned fruit
½   cup water
2   tablespoons white rice vinegar
2   tablespoons sugar
½   teaspoon salt

1   tablespoon cornstarch, dissolved in 2 tablespoons cold water

6   canned pineapple slices, cut in half

ON THE TRAY:
Bottle of peanut oil
Cup containing onion
Bowl containing sauce
Bowl containing duck meat
Cup containing cornstarch
Pineapple slices

TO COOK:

To a heated wok add 2 tablespoons peanut oil. When oil is hot, add onion and stir-fry 1 minute. Add sauce and stir until it boils. Add duck meat and stir until it is heated through. Add cornstarch and stir about 1 minute until the sauce is thickened. Remove from the heat.

TO SERVE:

Arrange pineapple slices on a large, deep platter. Pour duck meat and sauce over the pineapple slices. Serve immediately. This dish can be made with leftover chicken or turkey.

MAIL-ORDER SOURCES

If you have been unable to find some of the Chinese food ingredients or equipment you want, here are companies from which you can order by mail. These companies will supply you, on request, with current lists of the items they have available and their prices.

FOR FOODS AND INGREDIENTS

East Wind
2801 Broadway
New York, New York 10025

Star Market
3349 N. Clark Street
Chicago, Illinois 60657

FOR EQUIPMENT:

The Greens Farms Bookstore
1254 Post Road
Westport, Connecticut 06880

Star Market
3349 N. Clark Street
Chicago, Illinois 60657

INDEX

(Page numbers in boldface indicate where the recipes actually appear.)

A

Advance Preparation Schedule, 57
  See also schedules following Menu
    Lessons 1–6
Agar-Agar, 24
  Salad, 197, 198, **204**
Almond Cookies, 91, 92, 93, **102**, 104
Almond Float, 78, 79, 80, **88**, 90
Almond Fried Rice, 173, 174, **177**
Almond Junket. *See* Almond Float
Anise, Star. *See* Star Anise
Ants Climbing a Tree, 50, 155, **157**
Appetizers
  Barbecued Spareribs, 51, 70, 71, **72**,
    77
  Batter-Dipped Crabmeat, **233**
  Cold Drunken Chicken, 51, 188, **189**
  Egg Rolls, 78, 79, **81**, 90, 217

Fried Butterfly Shrimp, 188, 189,
    190
  Fried Dumplings, 106, **220**
  Fried Won Tons with Sweet and
    Sour Sauce, 95, 180, **181**
  Paper-Wrapped Chicken, 166, **167**
  Pearl Balls, 39, 205, **206**
  Shrimp Balls, 160, **161**
  Shrimp-Stuffed Mushrooms in Oys-
    ter Sauce, 91, 93, **94**, 104
  Shrimp Toast, 105, 106, **107**, 116
  Sliced Fragrant Beef, 51, 117, 118,
    121, 134
  Spring Rolls, **217**
  Steamed Beef Dumplings, 33, 105,
    106, **108**, 116
  Tea Eggs, 117, 118, **120**, 134
Asparagus, Stir-Fried, **226**